JOSÉ MOURINHO

FIFTY DEFINING FIXTURES

JOSÉ MOURINHO

FIFTY DEFINING FIXTURES

Tony Matthews

AMBERLEY

First published 2014

Amberley Publishing
The Hill, Stroud
Gloucestershire, GL5 4EP

www.amberley-books.com

British Library Cataloguing in Publication Data.
A catalogue record for this book is available from the British Library.

ISBN 978 1 4456 4230 7 (print)
ISBN 978 1 4456 4250 5 (ebook)

Typesetting and Origination by Amberley Publishing.
Printed in the UK.

Contents

About the Author

Tony Matthews, born and bred in the Black Country, was a semi-professional footballer in Switzerland and assisted several English clubs before becoming a PE/sports coach.

Player-manager of West Bromwich Albion Old Stars for a decade (1979–89), he was engaged as Albion's official statistician for over thirty years, and is now regarded as a prolific author/co-compiler of football books, with over 130 produced to date, his first in 1974.

Tony, who has run two marathons and once owned a personal collection of 1 million football programmes, is now sports reporter for a local radio station and English-printed newspaper in Spain, and over the last decade has helped raise over £100,000 for various charities.

Stats

Personal Information

Full name: José Mário dos Santos Mourinho Félix
Date of birth: 26 January 1963
Place of birth: Setubal, Portugal
Playing position: Central midfield
After retiring as a player: Interpreter, assistant manager, coach, manager

Playing Career

Seasons	Clubs	Apps	Goals
1979/80	Os Belenenses	0	0
1980–82	Rio Ave	16	2
1982/83	Os Belenenses	16	2
1983–85	Sesimbra	35	1
1985–87	Comérico e Indústria	27	8
(Eight seasons	Four clubs	94	13)

*Club appearances and goals are for the domestic League competitions only.

Clubs after Retiring as a Player

Season	Club	Position
1992/93	Sporting Clube de Portugal	Interpreter/Assistant Manager
1993–96	FC Porto	Interpreter/Assistant Manager
1996–2000	CF Barcelona	Interpreter/Assistant Manager
2000/01	Benfica	Manager
2001/02	União de Leiria	Manager
2002–04	FC Porto	Manager
2004–07	Chelsea	Manager

2008–10	Internazionale	Manager
2010–2013	Real Madrid	Manager
2013–present	Chelsea	Manager

Trophies Won as Manager

- Champions League: 2004, 2010
- UEFA Cup: 2003
- Premier League: 2005, 2006
- FA Cup: 2007
- League Cup: 2005, 2007
- FA Community Shield: 2005
- Portuguese Liga: 2003, 2004
- Portuguese Cup: 2003
- Portuguese Supertaça Cândido de Oliveira: 2004
- Supercoppa Italiana: 2008, 2010
- Italian Serie A: 2009, 2010
- Coppa Italia: 2010
- Spain's Cup del Rey: 2011
- Spain's Primera/La Liga: 2012
- Supercopa de España: 2012

Record: Twenty trophies in twenty-one years

BBC Sports Personality of the Year, December 2005

After guiding Chelsea to the Premiership title in 2004/05 – the first time the Blues had finished top of the English First Division/Premiership for fifty years, since their triumph in 1954/55 – José was voted the 'BBC Sports Personality Coach of the Year'.

The Portuguese 'Special One' was chosen ahead of contenders such as England cricket coach Duncan Fletcher, Liverpool football boss Rafael Benitez and the Welsh Rugby Union chief Mike Ruddock.

'It is a great honour for me,' said José, after picking up his award, adding, 'Of the other three contenders they also deserve it and I think the success of this last year belongs to my two families – the family I have at home and the family I have at Stamford Bridge.'

Introduction

José Mário dos Santos Mourinho Félix, O. I. H., universally known in the football world as José Mourinho is regarded by many, to be one of the greatest managers of all time, even surpassing Sir Alex Ferguson.

He was born into a large middle-class family in Setúbal, Portugal, in January 1963. His father was José Manuel Mourinho Félix, who was generally referred to as Félix Mourinho, and his mother was Maria Júlia Carrajola dos Santos.

José's father was a professional footballer, serving with Os Belenenses and Vitória de Setúbal, and also gaining one full international cap for Portugal in the course of his career.

José's mother was a primary school teacher from an affluent background. Indeed, her uncle funded the construction of the Vitória de Setúbal football stadium.

Unfortunately, the dramatic fall of António de Oliveira Salazar's Estado Novo regime in April 1974 led to the family losing all but a single property in nearby Palmela.

Football, however, still played a major part in the life of the Mourinho family, and commitments in Porto and Lisbon meant that father Félix was often separated from his young son.

Once he had become a teenager, José travelled, whenever possible, to attend his father's weekend matches, and when his father retired to become a coach, he began observing training sessions and assessing opposing teams. He was so keen – a true football fanatic.

From the outset, when he knew what the game was all about, José insisted that he wanted to follow in the footsteps of his father by becoming a professional footballer, and this is precisely what happened.

A central midfielder, he joined the youth set-up at Clube de Futebol Os Belenenses in Lisbon. He slowly graduated through the ranks to the senior level, but failed to make the first team. There were far too many good players at the club around that time.

Retirement at the Age of Twenty-Four

In the 1981/82 season, José played for Second Division side Rio Ave Futebol Clube, based in Vila do Cone in Northern Portugal, where his father was coach. He returned for a second spell with Os Belenenses for the 1982/83 campaign, and after assisting G. D. Sesimbra in his native city of Setúbal for two years – from May 1983 to May 1985 – he spent the next two seasons with Comercio e Industria, before announcing that he would not be pursuing a career as a player. He retired in the summer of 1987, at the age of just twenty-four.

It was evident that José was not cut out to be a professional footballer, and he admitted this himself, saying that he lacked the requisite pace and power, and chose to focus on becoming a football coach instead.

While he was still a teenager, José's mother enrolled him in a business school, but he upset his family by dropping out on his first day, deciding he would rather focus on sport, and chose to attend the Instituto Superior de Educação Física (ISEF), Technical University of Lisbon, to study sports science.

He did well and was allowed to go out with others to teach physical education at various schools. He had earned his PE diploma within five years, after receiving consistently good marks throughout an extended course.

After attending coaching courses held by the English and Scottish Football Associations, Andy Roxburgh, former Scotland manager, took note of the drive, enthusiasm and attention to detail of the young Portuguese, and stated publicly that he would 'go far in the game, and would become an exceptionally fine coach, even a manager'.

José sought to redefine the role of coach in football, by mixing coaching theory with motivational and psychological techniques.

In the summer of 1992, he became an interpreter/coach for Sir Bobby Robson at Sporting Clube de Portugal. A year later, having been upgraded to assistant manager, he moved with Robson to FC Porto. Four years later, in 1996, the Robson-Mourinho combo then switched over the border into neighbouring Spain, to take up similar positions with CF Barcelona.

They did wonders at the Camp Nou together, and won the Copa Del Rey twice – in 1997, and again in 1998. The team doubled up in 1997, lifting the European Cup Winner's Cup as well. But then Robson left the Camp Nou to take over at PSV Eindhoven, leaving José to contemplate his own future.

Into the Benfica Hot Seat

He stayed on with Barcelona for another three years, acting as assistant manager to Dutchman Louis van Gaal. He certainly learnt an awful lot about the game (from Messrs Robson and van Gaal), and in the summer of 2000 he finally became a football club manager himself, appointed head coach of Benfica, taking over from Jupp Heynkes.

Unfortunately, his reign as boss of the Lisbon club lasted for just nine matches, played between 19 September and 5 December.

In fact, Benfica's performances out on the pitch had improved dramatically under José and, after a 3-0 victory over the reigning Portuguese champions Sporting Lisbon, José demanded an extension to his contract after threats to his job by new president Manuel Vilarinho. Vilarinho, it is understood, favoured historic manager António José Conçeicão Oliveira (known as Toni), who, in fact, was in his third spell as boss.

Vilarinho didn't yield and José resigned.

Out of football for a relatively short period of time, he returned to the game before the end of the year, and subsequently guided perennial strugglers União de Leiria to a seventh-place finish in the Portuguese First Division, which gave them a European adventure courtesy of the Intertoto Cup the following season.

FC Porto had taken note of the young manager's talents and, after making a desperately poor start to the 2002/03 season, they stepped in and signed José as their new manager.

FC Porto then stormed to the Portuguese Primiera Liga title, winning it in style by an astonishing eleven points above runners-up Benfica, his former club. FC Porto also lifted the Taça de Portugal, beating another of José's old clubs, União de Leiria, 1-0 in the final. For good measure, they completed the treble by defeating Celtic 3-2 in the UEFA Cup final in Sevilla. And all this happened in his first season – what an achievement.

Almost inevitably, the 2003/04 campaign yielded more success, with yet another treble, as FC Porto retained the Primiera Liga crown, lifted the Supertaça Cândido de Oliveira and celebrated the club's most outstanding success ever by winning the prestigious Champions League trophy with a convincing 3-0 victory over AS Monaco in the final in Gelsenkirchen, Germany.

This was the first time a club from Portugal had lifted the coveted European/ Champions League prize since 1987 when, by sheer coincidence, the same club, FC Porto, beat Bayern Munich.

Immediately after this triumph, José was heralded as a genius and, with all this worldwide fame to contend with, he was understandably a 'wanted man', and it was Chelsea who came calling in May 2004.

Negotiations were short and sweet, and José had no hesitation in taking over as manager at Stamford Bridge, becoming the London club's fourth foreign boss in a row, following in the footsteps of Ruud Gullit, Gianluca Vialli and Claudio Ranieri.

Three-Year Deal with Chelsea

José officially signed a three-year contract at Stamford Bridge in June 2004, in the presence of Russian multi-billionaire owner Roman Abramovich, who had bought Chelsea football club for £150 million in July 2003, and the Blues' chief executive Peter Kenyon. Like a duck to water, José settled in at his new home immediately, and this, I believe, is when he told the British press that he was 'The Special One' … although he probably heard a fan, a journalist, even a player, use that nickname while he was with FC Porto.

Already described as being charismatic and outspoken, José was his own man and he knew straight away which positions needed strengthening in the team. Within a matter of weeks, he had signed striker Didier Drogba from Olympique Marseilles for £24 million, and brought in the experienced Portuguese trio of defenders, Paulo Ferreira, Ricardo Carvalho and midfielder Tiago Mendes, to boost his squad.

His first Premiership game in charge couldn't have been any tougher, with Manchester United the visitors to Stamford Bridge, but Eidur Gudjohnsen's goal was enough to secure a 1-0 win, ensuring the Blues' fans instantly took the self-appointed 'Special One' to their hearts.

Chelsea won six of their first eight Premiership games under José. They drew the other two, before losing 1-0 at Manchester City, whose goal came from a Nicolas Anelka penalty. This would be the only time José, and Chelsea, would suffer a League defeat all season. What a start to your managerial career in England!

José settled on his favoured system of 4-3-3 after just one-and-a-half games in charge. Most of the time, he chose either Drogba or Gudjohnsen to lead the line, and they were outstanding, receiving plenty of crosses, high and low, from wingers Damien Duff and Dutchman Arjen Robben, who were asked to hug the flanks as often as possible.

Frank Lampard, Claude Makélélé and Tiago proved to be inspirational in midfield, while goalkeeper Petr Cech was solid and consistent behind a mean defence, which was marshalled impeccably by John Terry, alongside the impressive Portuguese import Carvalho. In fact, Chelsea's back line was virtually impenetrable, as solid as a rock.

José's first trophy was secured in February 2005, when Chelsea beat Liverpool 3-2 after extra time in the Carling League Cup final at the Millennium Stadium in Cardiff. Unfortunately, before this triumph, his team had been knocked out of the FA Cup, ousted by Newcastle United 1-0 in the fifth round at St James' Park. However, they were still going strong in both the Premiership and Champions League, having topped Group H, ahead of FC Porto, CSKA Moscow and Paris Saint-Germain.

Arguably the toughest game of the season was against Blackburn Rovers at Ewood Park, in early February 2005. Rovers, managed by former Chelsea player Mark Hughes, tried every trick in the book to upset the Blues' passing flow, with Robben in particular being on the end of several wild challenges, one quite outrageous. 'It was a horror challenge – very, very nasty,' said José.

But the Dutch winger had already done the damage, scoring the only goal of the game in the fifth minute. And how the players and travelling supporters celebrated at the final whistle!

Important away wins followed at Everton (1-0), Norwich City (3-1) and Southampton (3-1). West Bromwich Albion (1-0), Crystal Palace (4-1) and Fulham (3-1) were all beaten at home, and both Birmingham City (1-1) and Arsenal (0-0) earned creditable draws at Stamford Bridge.

Title Clinched at Bolton

On 30 April 2005, with just four Premiership games remaining, Chelsea travelled north to take on Bolton Wanderers at the Reebok Stadium. They knew that victory would bring them their first top flight League title for half a century – since the likes of Ken Armstrong, Frank Blunstone, Roy Bentley, Ron Greenwood, Eric Parsons, Bill Robertson and others won the old First Division back in 1954/55.

After a stuttering first-half performance, Frank Lampard put the seal on a magical day by scoring twice in the space of 16 minutes (60–76), to ensure José won the championship in his first season in English football – another truly remarkable achievement. And victory at Bolton also ensured the League and League Cup double for in-form Chelsea, who by now had knocked both Barcelona and Bayern Munich out of the Champions League, and had been held 0-0 at home by Liverpool in the first leg of the semi-final of this prestigious competition.

A strict disciplinarian, José insisted that his players' celebrations were kept fairly low-key, given the fact they had to contest the second leg of their Champions League semi-final against Liverpool at Anfield on the following Wednesday. Yet luck was with the Merseysiders that night, as Luis García's highly controversial goal sent Rafael Benitez's team through to the final in Istanbul. Chelsea were stunned, and José wasn't too pleased either.

The 2004/05 season was Chelsea's ninetieth in League football, their thirteenth consecutive campaign in the Premier League, and the ninety-ninth since the club was formed in 1905/06. And as stated, José Mourinho celebrated his first year in charge of the Blues handsomely with the Premier League and League Cup double.

The season was also notable for several other records that were set during the course of the campaign:

(a) fewest goals conceded in a Premier League season (fifteen – just six at home)
(b) most clean sheets kept in a season (twenty-five)
(c) most wins registered in a League season (twenty-nine)
(d) most consecutive away wins (nine)
(e) most points gained in a full top flight season of League football (ninety-five –
the overall record is ninety-nine in Division Two, achieved in 1988/89)

Michael Essien, Asier Del Horno and wide man Shaun Wright-Phillips were three new players brought in by José prior to the start of his second season in charge (2005/06), and he also recalled striker Hernan Crespo from his loan spell with Italian giants AC Milan.

However, after that highly successful first season in English football, José clearly knew that retaining the title would be an even tougher task than winning it for the first time, but he was confident that Chelsea could once again go all the way.

After Chelsea had started well by lifting the FA Community Shield – beating London rivals Arsenal 2-1 – José saw his team get off to a flying start in the Premiership, winning the first nine games, and not conceding a single goal in the opening seven. Indeed, they won ten and drew one of their first eleven encounters.

Of these victories, the best were against West Bromwich Albion (4-0), Bolton Wanderers (5-1), Liverpool (4-1 at Anfield), Tottenham Hotspur (2-0 at White Hart Lane), Arsenal (1-0 at Stamford Bridge) and 1-0 against newly promoted Wigan Athletic. In fact, it was the recalled and revitalised Argentinian Crespo who sealed the points for José's Chelsea, on the opening day of the Premiership season, scoring with a stunning effort in the very last minute to beat Wigan at the JJB Stadium.

When defeat eventually did arrive – a 1-0 reverse against Manchester United at Old Trafford in early November, Darren Fletcher scoring in the thirty-first minute – Chelsea reacted with typical fortitude, going on another convincing and solid winning run that covered another thirteen Premiership games. This included an away League triumph over Arsenal, their first in more than fifteen years, in what proved to be the club's last ever visit to Highbury. Victory over the Gunners also brought Chelsea the double over their London rivals.

The Blues also defeated Newcastle United (3-0 at home), Portsmouth (2-0 at Fratton Park for another double), Manchester City (1-0 at the City of Manchester Stadium, courtesy of Joe Cole's seventy-ninth minute winner), Wigan (1-0 to complete the double over the Hatters), Fulham (3-2 at home), Birmingham City (2-0, also at Stamford Bridge), West Ham United (3-1 at Upton Park), Sunderland (2-1 at The Stadium of Light) and Liverpool (2-0 at home), the latter two ensuring two more doubles.

However, it wasn't all success as Chelsea's Champions League campaign hit the skids in February, when they succumbed to a 3-2 aggregate defeat at the hands of José's former club, Barcelona, in the second round.

It was business as usual, though, in the Premiership, and while Chelsea suffered defeats away at Middlesbrough (0-3) and Fulham (0-1), they still continued to score plenty of goals against West Ham United (4-1), Everton (3-0), Tottenham Hotspur (2-1), Manchester City (2-0) and Bolton Wanderers (2-0). These teams were all swept aside as José maintained an attacking line-up that had opposing defenders shaking in their boots.

Back-to-Back Titles

A resounding 3-0 win for the now hard-to-beat Blues at home to Manchester United, at the end of April, secured back-to-back Premiership titles for José's side. The players celebrated by embarking on a lap of honour around the pitch. An ecstatic José tossed his championship medal into the cheering crowd, gathered in the Matthew Harding stand, undoubtedly making the day even more special for one delighted supporter.

Chelsea fans mostly admitted that the football produced by José's team in 2005/06 didn't always thrill to the degree it had the season before, but no one really cared in the end when they knew that the Championship trophy would be staying at Stamford Bridge for another year.

Unfortunately, José had numerous run-ins with the football authorities in 2005/06. The most high-profile case came with the Ashley Cole 'tapping up' affair, while he accused Swedish referee Anders Frisk of bias in a Champions League game against Barcelona – a move that resulted in the official subsequently announcing his retirement. There were also his controversial clashes with the press, many of which certainly provided much amusement and entertainment.

In the summer of 2006, José brought in the experienced German midfielder Michael Ballack from Bayern Munich, and the Ukrainian striker Andriy Shevchenko for £29.5 million from AC Milan; they had, at the time, almost 150 full caps between them. At the same time, he allowed both Duff and Gudjohnsen to move to pastures new. And the aforementioned Ashley Cole was also signed from Arsenal as part of a swap deal involving defender William Gallas at the end of August.

On the whole, 2006/07 turned out to be another impressive season for Chelsea. But early 2-1 defeats against Middlesbrough and London rivals Tottenham Hotspur, both away, meant José's side was always chasing Manchester United. After losing 2-0 at Liverpool in January, Chelsea remained unbeaten for the rest of the season, but the Old Trafford Reds bounded along regardless, and went on to win the title by six points. With important players such as goalkeeper Cech and centre-back Terry missing due to injury at various times, José talked of playing 'survival football'. It didn't work. In fact, Chelsea drew their last five Premier League games, dropping ten points in total – in the end they lost the title race by just six. Might the team have done better? Some say yes … José said no.

More disappointment was suffered in Europe where, once again, Chelsea were beaten by a new Cup 'bogey' team, Liverpool, in the semi-final of the Champions League, the tie being decided by a penalty shoot-out after a 1-1 aggregate draw. However, José's instinctive knack to get his hands on more silverware continued.

He did, however, certainly get his players all revved up and in peak condition before sending them out to beat Arsenal 2-1 in the 2007 League Cup final at Cardiff's Millennium Stadium. In the first FA Cup final to be staged at the new Wembley Stadium, he masterminded a tactical 1-0 triumph over the bookies' favourites Manchester United, courtesy of Didier Drogba's dramatic winner, with four minutes of extra time remaining at the end of a mammoth, breathtaking season. So it was another two more trophies in the boardroom cabinet at Stamford Bridge, plus two runners-up prizes and a semi-final defeat. Not at all bad really.

Fourth Season in Charge

Chelsea began the 2007/08 season (the fourth under José's charge) in a rather solid, if unspectacular, fashion. New arrivals at the 'Bridge' included Florent Malouda, Claudio Pizarro, Tal Ben-Haim and Steve Sidwell. They all seemed to be rather low-key signings in comparison to what had transpired during the previous summers, although he did sell winger Arjen Robben to Real Madrid for a record fee of £24 million. A few fans weren't too happy when they heard this had happened.

Two scruffy, and rather unimpressive, early wins over Birmingham City and Reading ensured a decent start to the 2007/08 season. Overall, though, performances had been flat, and when Chelsea lost 2-0 away at Aston Villa, rumours were beginning to circulate that all was not well in the José household.

Those who thought that things were somewhat uneasy at the 'Bridge' were proved right when, soon after a 1-1 home draw with Rosenborg in the Champions League, José packed his bags and surprisingly (to some) left Chelsea by mutual consent.

His spectacular tenure as Chelsea manager came to an abrupt end in September after it was reported that there had been a bust-up involving certain members of the board, which, by all accounts, stemmed from a breakdown in his relationship with skipper John Terry.

But the fans were left with the satisfaction of knowing that for two seasons their team, with José Mourinho at the helm, was indisputably the best in the land by a mile.

Soon after leaving Stamford Bridge, José was approached by the Football Association regarding the position of head coach. He was asked if he would consider taking over from Steve McClaren. But after consultation with his wife, José turned down the offer. He said later that he regretted not accepting the position.

After a fairly long period out of the game – around nine months, in fact – José returned to football in June 2008 as manager of top Italian Serie A club Internazionale, taking over from Roberto Mancini, who would later become boss of Manchester City.

Within three months, he had collected his first Italian honour, seeing Inter beat AS Roma 6-5 on penalties (after a 2-2 draw) to lift the Supercoppa Italiana. He then successfully guided Inter to the Serie A title, with AS Roma three points behind in second place. He also took Inter to the final of the Supercoppa, but this time he and his team had to settle for the runners-up prize after Inter were defeated 2-1 by SC Lazio.

To win two trophies in your first season was no mean feat.

Magical Treble in Italy

In 2009/10, more success followed when José waved his magic wand again and Inter became the first Italian club to complete a magical treble, winning the Serie A title (again), this time by just two points from AS Roma, whom they also defeated 2-1 in the final of the Supercoppa Italiana, and lifting the UEFA Champions League with a memorable 2-0 victory over Bayern Munich in Spain. It was the first time that Inter had won the latter competition since 1965.

In 2010, he duly collected his first FIFA Ballon d'Or Best Coach Award after joining Ernst Happel, Ottmar Hitzfeld and Jupp Heynckes as one of only four coaches to have won the European Cup/Champions League with two different teams.

However, when Real Madrid came sniffing around in May 2010, José decided to follow his boyhood dream of managing in Spain. He moved to the Estadio Santiago Bernabéu shortly before the 2010 World Cup kicked off in South Africa.

With Real Madrid, José once again produced the goods, leading his team to three more trophies in double quick time, as he seemed to come up against his former employers Barcelona in every competition.

In 2011, Real won the Copa del Rey when they defeated Barcelona 1-0 in the final – their first victory in this competition since 1993. A year later, Real claimed the La Liga title with a record tally of 100 points. They also struck a total of 121 goals, as they finished nine points clear of Barça, against whom they lost in the Supercopa de España of 2011, going down 5-4 on aggregate after two excellent contests. And to cap it all, Real then won that same Supercopa de España competition, also in 2012, when they edged past Barça once again, this time on the away goal rule in a two-legged final, which finished level at 4-4.

That made it twenty trophies in twenty-one years with four different clubs, each one in a different country – a wonderful record in anyone's language.

Also in his three seasons at the Estadio Santiago Bernabéu, José saw Real take second spot in La Liga to Barcelona on two occasions: they finished four points behind their El Clásico rivals in 2011 (ninety-six to ninety-two) and trailed by a massive thirteen points in 2013 (ninety-four to eighty-one). They also lost to city neighbours Atlético Madrid 2-1 in the final of the Copa del Rey of 2013, and crashed out of the Champions League three times in succession at the semi-final stage – losing to their Spanish foe from Barcelona in 2011, to Bayern Munich on penalties in 2012, and to another Bundesliga side, Borussia Dortmund, in 2013.

After three years in sunny Spain, where he certainly made a lot of friends and also a few enemies (as always), José was persuaded to return and take up his former position at Stamford Bridge. In June 2013, he agreed a four-year contract with the club.

In his first season back in the hot seat, Chelsea finished third in the Premiership, qualifying for the Champions League in the process. But there was one significant fact about the 2013/14 campaign – it was the first time a club managed by the 'Special One' had not finished in any of the top two positions in the League they were playing in.

Chelsea had their moments in 2013/14. In the Premiership, they beat Arsenal 6-0 when they produced some breathtaking football, and demolished Tottenham Hotspur 4-0 at the 'Bridge'. They also defeated Liverpool 2-0 at Anfield (in what at the time was billed a championship decider) and West Ham United 3-0 at Upton Park. They fell at the fifth-round hurdle in both the League Cup at Sunderland, and in the FA Cup at Manchester City, before crashing out in the semi-final of the Champions League to a very good Atlético Madrid side over two legs.

During the summer of 2014, José released the names of the players who would not be part of his plans for the new campaign, and the list included veteran left-back Ashley Cole (who made 338 first-class appearances for the Blues), striker

Samuel Eto'o, reserve goalkeeper Henrique Hilario, legendary midfielder Frank Lampard and midfielder Sam Hutchinson.

On 1 June 2014, Lampard officially left Chelsea, after thirteen years at Stamford Bridge, during which time he scored a club record 211 goals in 648 appearances, and took his tally of full England caps to 106. He helped the Blues win thirteen trophies, including three Premier League titles, four FA Cup finals, two League Cup finals, one Europa League final and the European Champions League. A top man and certainly a top-class player, 'Lamps' subsequently signed for New York City to play in America's MLS.

Also out of the 'Bridge', in the summer of 2014, went Brazilian World Cup centre-back David Luiz, who was transferred to French club Paris Saint-Germain for £40 million, and forward Demba Ba, who was signed by the Turkish outfit Besiktas for £4.7 million. Experienced left-back Ashley Cole also left Stamford Bridge for a spell in Italy's Serie A.

Meanwhile, José boosted his squad by recruiting four vastly experienced internationals: Spanish striker Diego Costa from Atlético Madrid for £32 million; his fellow countryman and former Arsenal midfielder Cesc Fabregas from Barcelona for £30 million; the Brazilian left-back Filipe Luis Kasmirski, also from Atlético Madrid, for £15.8 million; and re-signing Chelsea's favourite son, Didier Drogba, who he persuaded to return for a second spell at Stamford Bridge after assisting Galatasaray in Turkey. The Ivorian international was officially given the No. 15 shirt.

José also recruited nineteen year old Croatian midfielder Mario Pasalic from Hajduk Split, who was immediately loaned out to FC Elche in La Liga to 'gain more experience'. Striker Loic Remy was signed from QPR for £10.5 million on transfer deadline day after Fernando Torres had been loaned out to Italian club AC Milan.

Chelsea started their 2014/15 Premiership programme with a trip to newly promoted Burnley on 18 August, and thereafter were scheduled to take on the 2014 Championship winners Leicester City (h), Everton (a), Swansea City (h), reigning champions Manchester City (a) and Aston Villa (h) before the end of September.

The first Premiership 'derby' of the season was marked down for 5 October, against Arsenal at Stamford Bridge. Might José and his players be on a roll once again? We will see.

SPORT LISBOA E BENFICA 1
OS BELENENSES 0
2 October 2000

José Mourinho was thirty-seven years of age when he recorded his first win as a football club manager in his third match, in charge of Benfica. Following a 1-0 defeat at the hands of Boavista in his first game, and a 2-2 home draw with Sporting Braga in his second, it was third time lucky for José when Benfica defeated his former club, Os Belenenses, by a goal to nil before an enthusiastic 25,000 crowd inside the 65,600 capacity Estadio da Luz in Lisbon.

Benfica (4-3-3): Enke, Rojas, Marchena, Ronaldo, Diego Luis, Meira, Chano, Miguel (Nunes), Poborksy, Sabry (Carlitos), Van Hooijdonk.
Belenenses (4-3-3): Aurelio, Cabral, Wilson, Filgueira, Henriques, Tuck (Cafu), Lito (Marcao), Cleber (Neca), Guga, Verona, Eliel.
Attendance: 24,992

Benfica centre-back Carlos Marchena Lopez decided this tight contest with a goal on thirty-two minutes. Prior to that, the action at both ends of the field, even in the middle, had not been all that good. There were far too many mistakes, and the respective goalkeepers were hardly troubled as a rather fussy, whistle-happy referee awarded several free-kicks for mediocre challenges.

Under the floodlights – one of the best sets in the world – Benfica certainly looked nervous during the opening half-hour, but once Marchena had broken the deadlock their overall play improved to a certain degree. In the end, José's team could, and should, have won by a much wider margin. Belenenses 'keeper Marco Aurelio saved well from the Czech Republic and former Manchester United winger Karel Poborksy, and he also did well to prevent Sebastian Cruzado Chano from finding the net. At the other end of the field Robert Enke, in the Benfica goal, reacted brilliantly to keep out a smart header from Augusto Santana Guga, and Wilson Silva fired narrowly wide 15 yards from goal.

José was happy enough with the result, but he did shrug his shoulders when saying (about his team's overall performance) 'This has to improve!'

CELTIC 2 FC PORTO 3
(after extra time)
21 May 2003

José Mourinho celebrated his first season as a manager by winning three trophies with FC Porto, one of them being the 2003 UEFA Cup, when the Portuguese club beat Celtic in a five-goal thriller in Sevilla, Spain.

This was a cracking encounter, attended by almost 53,000 spectators, two-thirds of whom where clad in green and white and cheering on the Scottish club.

It was also the first game to use the silver goal rule, although it did not affect the outcome of the game – Porto scored in the second period of extra time – thus meaning that play had to continue for the duration of the full 120 minutes.

Prior to this game, no club from Scotland and Portugal had ever won the UEFA Cup, so this was another first as José's men triumphed on a magic night in Spain.

UEFA stated at the time that Celtic brought with them 'the largest travelling support to have assembled for a single game – around 80,000' and the green-and-white army spread all over Sevilla, packing bars, cafés and restaurants, as well as filling half of the Estadio Ramón Sánchez-Pizjuán, certainly conducted themselves admirably, despite seeing their favourites defeated. For their efforts, Celtic football club was presented with the FIFA Fair Play Award, which they collected with a formal recognition from UEFA at a home game the following season.

Celtic, the clear favourites to lift the 2003 UEFA Cup, had proved to be an honest, hard-working team under manager Martin O'Neill, but they came up against a FC Porto side well versed in the dark arts of European football.

En route to the final, Celtic had eliminated Suduva (10-1 on aggregate), Blackburn Rovers, Celta Vigo, Stuttgart, Liverpool (4-3 on aggregate) and Boavista in the semis, while José's men had knocked out FK Austria, FC Lens, Denizli, Panathinaikos and SC Lazio (4-1 on aggregate) in their semi-final.

Celtic (4-4-2): Douglas, Agathe, Thompson, Mjalby, Balde, Valgeren (Laursen), Lambert (McNamara), Lennon, Sutton, Larsson (2 goals), Petrov (Maloney).
FC Porto: (4-3-3): Vitor Baia, Paulo Ferreira, Nuno Valente, Costinha (Ricardo Costa), Jorge Costa (Pedro Emanuel), Deco, Alenichev, Capucho (Marco Ferreira), Derlei, Maniche.
Attendance: 52,972

The game itself was a slow burner, which burst into life as the minutes rolled by. After a hectic first half, which saw tempers flare, the basic football technique was missing for long periods. Then, after a half-time chat (from both managers), the sparks and fireworks started to fly at both ends of the field.

The atmosphere inside the Estadio Olimpico throughout the final was as good as it gets – noise without nastiness, passion without bust-ups. And it was Porto who had just clinched their nineteenth Portuguese League title and, with a twenty-seven-week unbeaten run behind them, who started the better. Celtic, pipped by Glasgow rivals Rangers by one point in the race for the SPL crown, couldn't get out of their own half, and with the early stages of the final being marred by several heavy challenges, Celtic's Joos Valgaeren was the first player to be cautioned for a desperate lunge at Luis Da Souza (commonly known as Deco).

When the over-physical side subsided, Porto began to show their class, with Deco impressing in midfield. They were superior in technique, but looked vulnerable to crosses into their area.

After some rather negative attacking play (from both teams), halfway through the first half, Celtic's Swedish star Henrik Larsson tested Vitor Baia with a 25-yard free-kick, while at the other end Nuno Capucho went close for Porto. And it was the Portuguese club who scored first; Deco's close control and tricky footwork set up Dmitri Alenichov, whose drive was pushed out by keeper Rab Douglas straight to Brazilian Vanderiei Derlei, who netted on the stroke of half-time.

Tempers rose again in the tunnel, with an unsightly bout of pushing and shoving involving players and coaches alike, sparked when Derlei unsportingly kicked the ball into the stomach of Celtic's Didier Agathe.

Within two minutes of the restart, Celtic drew level when Larsson exploited Porto's frailty in the air. From Agathe's deep cross from the right, Larsson – lurking at the far post – sent a looping header over Baia for his 200th goal for the club.

However, Celtic's joy was short-lived. In the fifty-fourth minute, Deco beat two opponents with ease, to tee up the unmarked Alenichev, who steered the ball past Douglas from 12 yards.

Then, two minutes later, after some anxious moments and slack marking in Porto's penalty area, Larsson made it 2-2 with a free header from Alan Thompson's right-wing corner. Game on, and the second half was proving to be as exciting as the opening forty-five minutes were tedious, with players charging around at a frantic pace despite the heat.

Chances became scarce after this, and although both goalkeepers had to collect harmless looking crosses and field long-range efforts, the game went to an extra thirty minutes.

Unfortunately, Celtic defender Bobo Balde was sent off six minutes into the first period of extra time, giving Porto the advantage. They grabbed the winner through Derlei in the 115th minute. Plucky Celtic were powerless to respond, even when Porto's Nuno Valente was dismissed late on.

Man for man, the Portuguese champions were certainly superior but Celtic's passion and never-say-die attitude made them a match for José Mourinho's side.

However, this victory was a slap in the face for the Scots, and the world in general, and Porto's overall performance clearly showed the lengths a side managed by Mourinho would go to in pursuit of victory.

Porto, and their then relatively unknown head coach, would go on to bigger and better things, turning Mourinho into the 'Special One' and sending him on a personal crusade around Europe over the next decade.

Though O'Neill would win one more Scottish title in 2003/04 (his third in his five seasons in Glasgow), this was surely the highlight of his time at Celtic, even if it ended without a trophy.

FC PORTO 3 AS MONACO 0
26 May 2004

For the first time in fourteen years – since Benfica played AC Milan in 1990 – a Portuguese club had reached the European Cup final, and no team from Portugal had lifted the coveted trophy since FC Porto themselves had triumphed in 1987.

This was an epic achievement for José Mourinho, following his success twelve months earlier in the UEFA Cup final when FC Porto defeated Celtic.

On their way to the final, José's team won three of their Group F matches – 1-0 at home and 3-2 away v. Olympique Marseille and 2-1 v. Partizan Belgrade – drew two, both 1-1 in Belgrade and at home to Real Madrid (and lost one 3-1 at home to Real). They finished second behind the Spanish club. Then, entering the knockout stages, Porto ousted Manchester United over two legs, winning 2-1 at home and drawing 1-1 at Old Trafford, courtesy of a dramatic ninetieth minute equaliser from Costinha.

In the quarter-finals, FC Porto beat the French club Lyon 4-2 on aggregate (gaining a 2-0 victory at home and a 2-2 draw in the return leg away) before eliminating La Coruna in the semi-finals. They were held 0-0 at home, but won 1-0 in Spain thanks to Derlei's sixtieth minute penalty.

AS Monaco knocked out José's future club, Chelsea, in their semi-final, having earlier accounted for Arsenal and having initially topped Group C.

Described in the informative Champions *magazine as 'the essence of the thinking girl's crumpet and boasting confidence just a little short of arrogance' at the age of forty-one, José Mourinho had reached the high peak of his career, as his personal pulling power propelled his players to a comprehensive victory over the French champions in the final in Gelsenkirchen, Germany.*

FC Porto (4-2-1-3): Vitor Baia, Paulo Ferreira, Nuno Valente, Carvalho, Costinha, Jorge Costa, Pedro Mendes, Deco (Pedro Emanuel), Carlos Alberto (Alenichev), Derlei (McCarthy), Maniche.
AS Monaco (4-3-3): Roma, Ibarra, Zikos, Givet (Squillaci), Evra, Rodriguez, Cisse (Nonda), Bernardi, Giuly (Prso), Morientes, Rothen.
Attendance: 53,053

The Monegasque club AS Monaco, playing in their first European final, were favourites with the bookies and, led by captain Ludovic Giuly, who took up a central attacking position, they opened strongly. Indeed, on four occasions in the opening three minutes, Giuly's pace nearly caught Porto cold but the experience of his opposite number, Jorge Costa, was enough to keep him at bay three times as he darted towards the penalty area. And, with Monaco pressing hard, Lucas Bernardi's searching pass was collected by Giuly, but thankfully goalkeeper Vítor Baía raced out of his 6-yard area to effect a risky last-ditch tackle.

Giuly was playing superbly, showing some deft touches in and around the Porto penalty-area. On fifteen minutes, he set up Édouard Cissé, whose cross was tantalisingly out of reach of Bernardi's outstretched leg. Soon afterwards he provided Jérôme Rothen with a chance to cross from the other flank, but this time striker Fernando Morientes was just out of range.

Unfortunately for Monaco, it was to be nothing more than a cameo from their captain, who took a hefty challenge in centre-field and limped off after just twenty-two minutes, clutching his midriff, handing the armband to Julien Rodriguez and being replaced by Dado Prš.

Undeterred, Monaco kept up the momentum. Nuno Valente became the first player to receive a yellow card after a clumsy foul on Cissé. Almost immediately, Morientes was then adjudged offside from another astute pass from Bernardi as the Porto defence back-pedalled.

On thirty-four minutes, and having hardly threatened the Monaco goal, the pendulum suddenly swung Porto's way when Rothen lost possession to Paulo Ferreira, who charged up the right flank before crossing to the near post. Rodriguez, timing his challenge to perfection, just beat Deco to the ball.

Five minutes later – perhaps against the run of play – Porto took the lead from the same source. This time right-back Paulo Ferreira's centre was a lofted one and it found Carlos Alberto. Unselfishly, he attempted to lay the ball off to Derlei but the ball bounced back to the teenager, off the hapless Akis Zikos, and this time it was thumped into the back of the Monaco net with aplomb, past Flavio Roma's left hand.

Up to that point, with the interval looming, Monaco had been by far the better side. During the opening period of the second half, they once again looked the better team, and as Porto failed to capitalise on their one-goal advantage, a second marginal offside verdict denied Morientes an equaliser.

On the hour mark, José withdrew Carlos Alberto in favour of Russian midfield player Dmitri Alenichev, and four minutes later Monaco brought on Shabani Nonda in place of Cissé, as the French champions threw caution to the wind.

But as their forays began to flounder on the edge of the Porto penalty area, chances of a decisive counter-attack grew more likely, and so it proved.

In the seventy-first minute, Deco broke clear of his shackles and found Alenichev on the left. The Russian slipped the ball straight back into the playmaker's path and the midfielder gleefully stroked home Porto's second.

Four minutes later it was game over. This time it was Derlei who broke free, and his angled cross found Alenichev thanks to a deflection off substitute

Sébastien Squillaci. Alenichev needed no second invitation and, seeing the sight of the Monaco goal, he let rip to drive a third nail in Monaco's coffin. Later on, both Derlei and his replacement, McCarthy, had efforts saved by Roma, while a deflated Monaco side created only more chances before Danish referee Nielsen blew the final whistle to bring joy and delight to the Porto bench, with José leading the celebrations. He continued to lap up the victory by running round the pitch, holding aloft the trophy with goalkeeper Vitor Baia and Jorge Costa.

Two days later, José – who by now had been dubbed 'the Mastermind Mauler of Monaco' – left FC Porto to take over as Chelsea boss.

CHELSEA 1 MANCHESTER UNITED 0
15 August 2004

José Mourinho's first Premier League game in charge of an English club resulted in a single-goal victory over Manchester United. At the same time, it earned the Blues their first back-to-back home wins over the Old Trafford Reds for thirteen years.

In a tight, hard-fought encounter of precious few chances, it was the boot of Icelandic international striker Eidur Gudjohnsen that made the crucial difference.

José handed debuts to five players – goalkeeper Petr Cech, full-back Paulo Ferreira, midfielder Alexeï Smertin and striker Didier Drogba – so it would have been a lot to ask for a performance of total cohesion and understanding, but José's side had just enough, both in determination and a certain amount of skill, to trouble the visitor's back line and grind out an important opening-day victory.

Chelsea (4-4-2): Cech, Ferreira, Gallas, Terry, Bridge, Gérémi (Carvalho), Makélélé, Lampard, Smertin, Drogba (Kezman), Gudjohnsen (Parker).
United (4-4-2): Howard, Silvestre, Neville, Keane, Fortune (Richardson), Miller (Bellion), O'Shea, Djemba-Djemba (Forlan), Giggs, Scholes, Smith.
Attendance: 41,813

The atmosphere inside the ground was electric, and those present saw a frantic opening to the game. An early half-chance fell to United's John O'Shea, but his header was off target. Soon afterwards, Alan Smith headed a deep cross from Ryan Giggs over the bar.

However, despite those early scares, it was Chelsea who made the breakthrough.

Fortune failed to make a clearance, and this allowed Gérémi to break with pace into the United half. He found enough space to send the ball into the danger-zone, where Drogba, towering above all around, headed it down to Gudjohnsen, who knocked it over the advancing Howard, before he rounded to run the ball home, with Roy Keane chasing back in vain.

A minute later, Drogba almost made it two, from Frank Lampard's pass, but this time Howard was able to dispossess as the striker attempted to go past him.

Giggs was causing a few problems and, just after the half-hour mark, Petr Cech and his defenders got in the way of each other from one of his high crosses and, soon afterwards, Paul Scholes drove wide. At the other end Drogba was also causing problems, particularly for Roy Keane in central defence and, when the Chelsea striker ran at him on the edge of the area, Keane stopped him with a blatant body check. Lampard struck the resulting free-kick 4 yards wide.

There was plenty of action during the opening stages of the second half, but goal-scoring chances were few and far between. Drogba sent one header over and Howard won a fifty-fifty chase with Gudjohnsen.

On sixty-nine minutes José, made his first substitution, bringing on fresh legs in the form of Mateja Kezman, who replaced Drogba. Three minutes later, United brought on Diego Forlan for Djemba-Djemba.

Almost immediately the game opened up, and Cech was sharp enough to smooth a Giggs effort while Forlan beat the offside flag, but blasted embarrassingly off target.

Chelsea had been forced back but defended well, although the visitors were sensing an equaliser.

On eighty minutes, Giggs evaded William Gallas to send Alan Smith's cross past the post from 10 yards out. At this juncture, José swapped striker Gudjohnsen with midfielder Scott Parker, leaving Kezman up front on his own.

The Chelsea boss then added Portuguese defender Ricardo Carvalho to the midfield battle, in place of the hard-working Gérémi, while David Bellion and Kieran Richardson came on for Liam Miller and Quinton Fortune as United went for broke with the minutes ticking by.

Very late on, Chelsea had two chances to make sure of the points. In the end, though, one goal was enough to give José his first ever win as manager of an English club.

José remarked after the game,

When Silvestre [United defender] said we haven't got the time to create a big team spirit, he was wrong. We were a team mentally today – and we had to win this match because of the three points we get against our direct opponent. And I think we deserved them because of the team spirit. If you have to play a little bit different to win a game, then you have to do it. But I have to say it's maybe a bit unfortunate for Manchester United to leave Stamford Bridge without a point. They played well, weren't afraid of us, and risked everything at 1-0 down. Mr [Alex] Ferguson pushed me to make changes that normally I don't do to play a safer match, and, in fact, the team defended very, very, very well. We have to work every day as I was saying. Manchester United and Arsenal have great teams, and have worked with their managers for a long time. We've been together for three weeks, but we have this spirit and organisation, and we play with maximum effort and quality at certain moments.

The Portuguese boss was impressed with the atmosphere generated by the fans at the game, saying,

I thought before the game 'this is an unbelievable atmosphere'.

In Portugal we have this a few times a year with Porto, Sporting Lisbon and Benfica. I think I'm a lucky person to work in the Premiership – and I want to stay as long as I can.

The Stamford Bridge website editor stated online: 'This was not yet a Chelsea team into full stride but, in the month of the Olympic Games, we have left the starting blocks well.'

PARIS SAINT-GERMAIN 0 CHELSEA 3
14 September 2004

Chelsea carved out a comfortable win over the French giants Paris Saint-Germain, in their opening Champions League Group H match. Afterwards José Mourinho said: 'It was a fantastic performance from the whole team.'

PSG had finished second to Lyon in 2003/04, missing out on the title by three points (79-76), whereas Chelsea had taken the runner's-up spot, behind Arsenal, in the Premiership.

PSG (4-3-3): Letizi, Mendy, Helder, Pierre-Fanfan, Armand, Ogbeche (Pancrate), M'Bami, Coridon (Ljuboja), Cana, Rothen (Ateba), Pauleta.
Chelsea (4-4-2): Cech: Ferreira, Gallas, Terry, Bridge, Tiago, Makélélé, J. Cole (Geremi), Lampard, Gudjohnsen (Kezman), Drogba (Duff).
Attendance: 49,543

José, looking for his second straight Champions League trophy, saw his Chelsea side get off to a positive start.

Frank Lampard floated in a couple of corners, but Eidur Gudjohnsen and Tiago's connecting headers were dealt with comfortably by the PSG defence.

In fact, it was the French side that created the first clear-cut chance at the Parc des Princes. Charles-Édouard Corridon surged forward from midfield but, although unchallenged, his attempted chip over 'keeper Petr Cech sailed wide.

In the tenth minute, Gudjohnsen suffered a deep cut over his eye, after cracking heads with José Pierre-Fanfan. The Iceland striker was replaced by Mateja Kezman.

With both teams adopting defensive tactics, the midfield was far too congested for the creative players to perform, and it was up to defenders William Gallas and John Terry to try their luck with long-range efforts, while Drogba was thwarted by PSG 'keeper Lionel Letizi.

The deadlock was finally broken in the twenty-eighth minute, when a horrible mistake by Letizi gifted Terry a simple headed goal. Letizi went for, and completely missed, a high swinging corner from Lampard, allowing the Chelsea skipper to head home from 8 yards. The goal injected new energy into the match and

Cameroon international Modeste M'Bami saw his low drive turned wide by Cech, who then smothered a shot from Lorik Cana.

Joe Cole was looking fluid and his skill was rewarded on the stroke of half-time, when he helped set up Drogba who then netted Chelsea's second goal. Letizi saved Kezman's initial effort, but only succeeded in pushing the ball into the path of Drogba who, unmarked, gleefully slid the ball home.

Chelsea continued to apply the pressure in the second-half, and Cole was twice denied, while Lampard saw his free-kick clear the bar by inches.

On fifty-two minutes, former Monaco star Jerome Rothen curled in a dangerous free-kick but Elber's header looped wide. Two efforts from the Portuguese striker Pauleta were easily dealt with by the impressive Cech.

With Drogba continuing to cause problems, it was no surprise when Chelsea grabbed a third goal in the seventy-fifth minute.

Kezman was fouled 1 yard outside the box by Elder and, from the free-kick, Drogba's right-footed drive zipped over the wall to leave Letizi helpless.

There was no way back for PSG, and Chelsea comfortably ran down the clock, stretching their unbeaten run for the season.

A smiling José said afterwards: 'That was good; we played very well and deserved to win – perhaps by more goals.'

MANCHESTER CITY 1 CHELSEA 0
16 October 2004

José's Mourinho's first League defeat as Chelsea's boss came in his ninth match, away at Manchester City (managed by Kevin Keegan). At the time, City were lodged halfway down the Premier League table while Chelsea, after six wins and two draws, were lying second behind their London neighbours and reigning champions Arsenal.

There were over 45,000 fans inside the City of Manchester Stadium, and those present saw the points decided early in the first half by a penalty. As a result, Chelsea suffered their first defeat in thirteen Premiership games against City, since October 1993.

Manchester City (4-4-2): James, Mills, Thatcher, Dunn, Distin, Bosvelt, Wright-Phillips, Sibierski, Jihai (McManaman), Anelka, Macken (Fowler).
Chelsea (4-4-2): Cech, Ferreira, Carvalho (Geremi), Terry, Gallas (Bridge), Lampard, Tiago (J. Cole), Makélélé, Gudjohnsen, Kezman, Duff.
Attendance: 45,047

After a fairly even opening period, when both sides tended to size each other up, some quick thinking by City's Paul Bosvelt brought about only the second goal Chelsea had conceded during the first quarter of the season. It came in the eleventh minute, on a pitch saturated by a torrential downpour just before kick-off.

In fact, the visitors were on the attack when William Gallas slipped and lost possession. Bosvelt instantly launched a long ball forward for the former PSG, Real Madrid, Liverpool and Arsenal striker Nicolas Anelka to exploit the lack of defensive cover. And with right-back Paulo Ferreira alone at the back, the French international burst into the penalty box, only to be wrestled to the ground by the one-time Porto defender. Referee Howard Webb had no hesitation in awarding a spot-kick, and was also lenient on Ferreira, allowing him to remain on the pitch by issuing him with a yellow card for his misdemeanour. Although, at the time, it looked a clear penalty, Ferreira protested that the first foul committed by him was outside the area, and after the game, TV footage confirmed this to be the case.

Unperturbed by almost a minute of arguments, Anelka, who would join Chelsea for £15 million in January 2008, as cool as a cucumber, flicked the penalty over Petr Cech's dive to put City in front.

Chelsea tried to hit back, but with Didier Drogba out of the team, their attack lacked penetration, although goalkeeper David James and his City defenders made typically hard work of dealing, with a couple of tempting crosses.

Chelsea struggled to get going in the first half and managed only three direct attempts on goal, all of them speculative shots, by Frank Lampard, Tiago and Gallas. Only Lampard's effort was on target. While in stoppage time, with the referee ready to blow his whistle to take the players off, a free-kick by the same Chelsea midfielder brushed Eidur Gudjohnsen on the way through, causing James to save with his legs. This was a close shave.

Although Chelsea were only mediocre, City never looked like extending their lead before the interval either. In fact, their only promising moment came when Sun Jihai hopefully picked out Antoine Sibierski at the far post, only to see the Frenchman make a complete hash of his volley. Jihai did not see much else after that, having to hobble off in pain after tackling Gudjohnsen and getting his leg caught under the Icelandic striker.

José Mourinho was furious with his players at half-time, and he remained furious with them afterwards. When 'keeper Cech booted a clearance straight into touch, the Chelsea boss bawled him out from his technical area, to the clear amusement of his counterpart Keegan nearby. The City fans in the main stand behind immediately mimicked his theatrical, raised-arms gesture. They enjoyed that so much they did it every time José expressed frustration, which was, in truth, often.

Chelsea did far better after the break. Lampard fired against a post from the edge of the area, before bringing a fine fingertip save from James, but Chelsea quickly slipped back into mediocrity and it was City who grew stronger as the game progressed. Despite having the lion's share of the ball, only Shaun Wright-Phillips came anywhere near to adding to their lead. The oft-criticised City back four looked a solid unit throughout the second half, and it was Bosvelt and Steve McManaman who were bossing midfield on their own at the end. It must be said that City actually toyed with Chelsea during the last fifteen minutes as the home crowd's applause rang round the stadium.

Indeed, as the minutes ticked on by, the City supporters took great delight in poking fun at the Chelsea manager's increasingly hysterical touchline histrionics, once his team proved incapable of responding to shipping that early goal.

This was not a situation José, or anyone else at Chelsea, could have been happy with, and the introduction of substitutes Joe Cole and Géremi made no difference whatsoever.

Despite the expensive overhaul and the extensive Portuguese influence, Chelsea lost a game they were expected to win. But that's football. Anything can happen when least expected. Things would improve.

CHELSEA 1 WEST HAM UNITED 0
26 October 2004

José Mourinho celebrated victory in his first domestic Cup game as Chelsea's manager. It wasn't the prettiest of wins, but it was a sweet one, especially as it came against London rivals West Ham United.

Dutch international Arjen Robben, who had been signed from PSV Eindhoven for £12.1 million in the summer, had a fine game and created several chances for his colleagues. The Serbian international Mateja Kezman struck the all-important match-winning goal twelve minutes into the second half.

Chelsea (4-4-2): Cudicini, Paulo Ferreira, Gallas, Carvalho, Babayaro, Tiago, Parker (Lampard), Geremi, Cole (Duff), Kezman, Robben.

West Ham United (4-4-2): Walker, Mullins, Ferdinand, Repka, Brevett, Etherington (Rebrov), Lomas, Nowland (Nolan), Reo-Coker, Harewood, Zamora (Hutchison).

Attendance: 41,774

Just twenty-four hours after football showed its dark side, with violent scenes at the Carling Cup game between Millwall and Liverpool in south-east London, the ugly face of the game erupted again at Stamford Bridge during this capital city derby.

The Metropolitan Police made eleven arrests inside the ground for various offences, including the possession of offensive weapons, drugs and violent disorder. One officer said, 'The majority of fans behaved and it was reasonably peaceful, but the yobs were there in force, once again!'

That was before the game. After the final whistle it got worse, when some 200 thugs went on the rampage in the Matthew Harding Stand. One West Ham fan was carried away on a stretcher, following a scuffle involving his colleagues and a group of Chelsea supporters, as flying missiles were directed at Hammers' fans by their counterparts from the East Stand.

Those who threw objects may have done so in a warped defence of Chelsea striker Mateja Kezman, who suffered a nasty head wound when he was struck by a bottle just as his teammate Frank Lampard, an ex-Hammer of course, prepared to take a penalty in front of them. 'I'm fine' said a dutifully tight-lipped Kezman, having seen the usually reliable Lampard miss from the spot, Jimmy Walker saving with his legs as the Chelsea man fired straight at the 'keeper.

José Mourinho treated this match so seriously that often it seemed a star-studded cast was employed, merely to help his misfiring striker find his feet in England. Three times the Serbian international had a golden opportunity to hit the target, but each time his first touch let him down. Thankfully, he could not squander sitters forever and, when Joe Cole created another chance with a smart through-ball, Kezman delivered, finding the net with a low shot, which went in off a post on fifty-seven minutes. This was the striker's first goal in thirteen appearances for the Blues. What a relief.

Chelsea's penalty was awarded fifteen minutes from time, following Tomas Repka's rash lunge at Robben but, alas, Lampard missed from 12 yards.

However, the midfielder almost made amends with a free-kick from wide on the left, which almost snapped the crossbar in two. The woodwork also denied a late powerful header by visiting defender Anton Ferdinand, as West Ham went for broke in the last ten minutes.

The first half was not brilliant. Carlo Cudicini, playing in place of Petr Cech, didn't see too much action but Robben, Geremi (with a rising 20 yarder) and Lampard all had opportunities to open the scoring at the other end of the field.

'It was probably a fair result', said West Ham's manager Alan Pardew, while the Chelsea website reporter stated, '1-0 or 8-0, it didn't matter. We progressed to the next round, where we've been given a tricky tie up at Newcastle. If we are to win our first piece of silverware since 2000, then this could be the game where it will matter.'

But if the truth be known, fans at this match did not talk about the football for long; it was the disgraceful scenes that went on between two rivals sets of hooligan supporters that was the focus of conversation.

NEWCASTLE UNITED 0 CHELSEA 2
(after extra time)
10 November 2004

This was a solid, hard-earned victory for Chelsea, who reached the last eight of the competition courtesy of a couple of classy finishes from two of their substitutes. Firstly, Eidur Gudjohnsen netted just four minutes after coming off the bench, while the second came from Arjen Robben with eight minutes remaining.

Marshalled superbly by John Terry, Chelsea's defence allowed the Magpies few chances, although the lively Laurent Robert twice went close with decent efforts.

Newcastle (4-4-2): Given, O'Brien, Bramble, Johnsen, Bernard (Hughes), Bellamy, Butt (Dyer), Jenas, Robert, Shearer, Kluivert (Ameobi).
Chelsea (4-1-4-1): Cudicini, Johnson, Terry, Gallas, Bridge, Paulo Ferreira, Tiago, Parker (Gudjohnsen), Duff (Robben), Kezman, Cole (Lampard).
Attendance: 38,055

Until Icelandic international Gudjohnsen's arrival, six minutes into extra time, Chelsea had played with just one striker, Serbian Mateja Kezman, though both Damien Duff and Joe Cole always tried to get forward in support.

Kezman, who had netted only one goal in fifteen appearances since his transfer from PSV Eindhoven, almost doubled that tally as early as the second minute. He pounced on Andy O'Brien's casual pass and slipped the ball past Shay Given, but from a tight angle was unable to guide his shot over the line.

That was Chelsea's best effort of the first half, though Glen Johnson selfishly shot from a difficult angle, much to the annoyance of both Duff and Kezman, who were well placed inside the box.

Not that Newcastle managed to create too many openings either. Indeed, during a fiesty first half, the hosts had three efforts on goal, their best chance falling to Olivier Bernard's shot, which was touched round a post by Carlo Cudicini.

Bernard also troubled the Chelsea 'keeper with an inswinging corner and between the action, four players – Cole, Tiago, Johnson and Nicky Butt – were all yellow-carded by efficient referee Steve Bennett.

Soon after the restart, Robert weaved his way into the Chelsea box, only to see his shot blocked by Scott Parker's excellent last-ditch tackle.

Late in the game, a swerving free-kick by Robert, who was by far Newcastle's best player, produced a splendid reaction save from Cudicini, who fisted the ball away.

On sixty-two minutes, another home defensive lapse – this one by Titus Bramble – almost let in Joe Cole, but the Newcastle player recovered to clear his lines.

Two minutes later, Cole and Kezman combined to free Tiago, only for the former Benfica midfielder to miss the target with only Given in front of him. The Newcastle number one also had to rush out of his box to hack the ball clear, as Arjen Robben threatened.

When the game moved into extra time, Chelsea took control and the goals from Gudjohnsen and Robben gave José's side their seventh successive victory.

Icelandic striker Gudjohnsen arrowed a shot past Given in the 100th minute. He allowed a Robben pass to run across him, before powering his shot into the net off the post.

Robben's goal was even better. He beat three players in a mazy dribble, which covered 50 yards, before side-footing the ball past Given into the far corner.

Chelsea, who had knocked West Ham United out in the third round, were rewarded with another London derby, this time against Fulham at Craven Cottage in the quarter-finals.

Later in the season, Chelsea would return to St James' Park to play Newcastle in a fifth round FA Cup-tie, but this time victory went to the Tyneside club by a goal to nil.

PREMIER LEAGUE
CHELSEA 1 EVERTON 0
6 November 2004

Chelsea went to the top of the Premier League with this hard-earned victory over third-placed Everton, at Stamford Bridge, with Arjen Robben netting the all-important goal with less than twenty minutes remaining.

Chelsea would remain top of the table until the end of the season – a prolonged period of six months, covering twenty-six more matches, during which time they remained unbeaten.

> **Chelsea** (4-4-2): Cech, Ferreira, Terry, Carvalho, Babayaro, Makélélé, Lampard, Tiago (Kezman), Robben, Duff (Huth), Gudjohnsen (Geremi).
> **Everton** (4-5-1): Martyn, Hibbert, Pistone (McFadden), Stubbs, Weir, Osman (Chadwick), Gravesen, Watson (Campbell), Bent, Cahill.
> **Attendance:** 41,965

After a tentative start, Chelsea gradually got the upper hand and, although Everton were dangerous on the break, it was the Blues of London who always looked the more threatening.

Chelsea fired on all cylinders and, since that hiccup against Manchester City the previous month, this was their sixth straight win in the space of eighteen days, seeing them catch up and subsequently overhaul Arsenal at the top of the Premiership, qualifying from their Champions League group and making steady progress in the Carling Cup.

Everton worked their socks off in an attempt to stretch the Division's best away record, which had previously yielded thirteen points from five games. But José's side clearly showed that they possessed patience and perseverance, as well as a lot of individual ability. After a rather moderate first-half performance, they prevailed after the break, with Arjen Robben following up his midweek winner against CSKA Moscow with a sublime finish to win the game and the points in the seventy-second minute.

The decisive move started deep in their own half of the field and gathered momentum when Eidur Gudjohnsen flicked the ball on for Robben, who dashed down the right flank. Holding off David Weir's challenge he cut inside, before lifting the ball over 'keeper Nigel Martyn, as he advanced from his line.

José, who had gone for broke by bringing on forward Mateja Kezman after the break, in an attempt to break the deadlock, said to reporter Stuart Barnes of the *Observer*,

> I told the players that if they want to become champions they must be prepared to take risks. We either live with that pressure, play risky football and just think about winning, or we just enjoy our life but have no trophies at the end of the season. Otherwise they could settle for a comfortable situation and an easy life. They kept faith. The dressing room was like it is after a Cup final, instead of just having gained three points. I can't take the credit for Robben because I didn't buy him. But what a player – we are a different team with him. He is fast, can beat people, works for the team and has a strong shot. It was not an easy week for us playing in Moscow and not getting enough sleep. It has been really difficult but the players showed a lot of character and desire.

Earlier in the season, José had accused Tottenham of 'parking a bus' in their penalty box to poach a point, but this time he clearly respected the resistance offered by Everton. 'They played a defensive game, but did it well', he said. 'They were strong, experienced and tough and made it difficult for us. But I thought we deserved what we got.'

Robben had earlier gone close with a vicious volley from 20 yards, which Martyn tipped onto the crossbar and over. But, for the most part, Chelsea's shooting was below par.

Frank Lampard, Damien Duff and Tiago all fired over from good positions, and Gudjohnsen wasted a golden opportunity by shooting into a crowd of players from six yards, following John Terry's clever knock-down.

Lampard was also denied a goal when his shot, following a corner, was blocked by stumbling Everton defender Alessandro Pistone, whose captain Alan Stubbs, was guilty of a glaring miss, heading Leon Osman's cross wide after Thomas Gravesen's short corner.

If Stubbs had scored, Everton would probably have won the game, but in the end it was Robben who stole the show.

Visiting manager David Moyes commenting on Chelsea, said,

> They are a very good team, but we kept them out and missed a good chance to make it 1-0. They were finding it difficult to break us down. If that chance had gone in from Stubbsy, who knows what would have happened. Their goal was probably the first time our midfield players were spread out. We just couldn't get back at Robben with his pace. He's such a good player, and if we had £12 million to spend we could buy someone like him. But you have to pay out what you can afford. If you can't shop at Armani you have to go to Marks & Spencer.

What an impact Robben made following his belated start to the season. He immediately gave Chelsea an extra dimension with his pace, vision and shooting power and his winning goal against Everton was the first of fifteen he would net for Chelsea in sixty-seven Premiership matches.

FC PORTO 2 CHELSEA 1
7 December 2004

Unfortunately, José Mourinho did not have a happy return to his former team. Porto, as the hosts, and holders of the trophy, scored a dramatic winner through Benni McCarthy, whose late header rescued the Portuguese club's Champions League campaign.

FC Porto had won their domestic League title by a mile in 2003/04, but had not made a great start to the new season. Chelsea, meanwhile, were playing well and looked confident of gaining a result in Portugal.

Porto (4-4-2): Nuno, Jorge Costa, Emanuel, Costinha, Fabiano (Postiga), Derlei (Quaresma), Areias, Diego (Peixoto), Maniche, Seitaridis, McCarthy.
Chelsea (4-4-1-1): Cech, Ferreira, Gallas, Terry, Carvalho, Smertin (Tiago), Lampard, Parker, Bridge, Duff (Robben), Drogba (Kezman).
Attendance: 42,409

Despite pre-match security concerns, smiling and waving, José was given a warm welcome to his former home by just over 42,000 fans in Portugal.

Having beaten Newcastle United 4-0 in the Premiership just seventy-two hours earlier, Chelsea's boss chose to delve into his strong squad for the return Champions League Group H game against Porto, making four changes to his line-up.

He brought in Alexei Smertin, Scott Parker, Wayne Bridge and Didier Drogba in place of Claude Makélélé, Arjen Robben, Eidur Gudjohnsen and Tiago.

Having lost 3-1 at Stamford Bridge at the end of September, Porto were desperate to carve out a win on home soil and held the initiative in the opening stages with their South African striker Benni McCarthy the main threat.

Yet it was Chelsea who posed the biggest danger on the break, mainly thanks to Damien Duff's pace down the wing.

After just three minutes, Wayne Bridge picked up the Irishman's cross from the right, but with his weaker right foot, he fired wide of the far post.

On twelve minutes, Frank Lampard combined with Duff on the overlap to feed the ball through to the waiting Drogba but goalkeeper Nuno, diving to his left, pushed the striker's close-range header onto the crossbar and away to safety.

However, a blunder by the Portuguese keeper in the thirty-third minute led to Chelsea taking a deserved lead. Duff, moving inside quickly at speed, zipped past full-back Pedro Emanuel and fired in a low shot from just inside the box. Nuno, well positioned, failed to get a full hand on the ball as it nestled into the bottom corner.

At this point, the home side had been restricted to set-piece chances as Chelsea slowly drew the sting from the game.

Diego came closest to the equaliser when Petr Cech had to punch his free-kick to safety but Chelsea kept their pattern and went in at the break, leading 1-0.

Early in the second half, some positive forward play suggested that Porto were going to make a fight of it, and this was emphasised when a shot from Diego in the fifty-eighth minute was blocked by Cech.

Two minutes later, the talented nineteen-year-old Brazilian breached Chelsea's stubborn defence.

Georgios Seitaridis saw his shot cleared by Chelsea skipper John Terry, but the ball fell nicely for Diego, who coolly found the net for the equaliser.

This goal lifted the tempo of the game, and José's Premiership leaders quickly took advantage of the space created by a more urgent Porto side.

After drifting past Jorge Costa, Drogba forced another good save from Nuno, before the hard-working Lampard was also denied by the Porto keeper in the seventy-second minute.

But then, just when it looked as if Chelsea would claim a draw, the home side stole victory with a last-gasp attack. Finding space on the left, Peixoto delivered an excellent cross in the eighty-sixth minute. McCarthy, rising above William Gallas inside the 6-yard box, found the net with a solid header.

The goal ensured Porto's title defence advanced to the knockout stages, and saw José's Chelsea fall to only their second defeat of the season.

CHELSEA 4 NORWICH CITY 0
18 December 2004

Ten days after losing narrowly in Portugal, and less than a week after drawing 2-2 with Arsenal at Highbury, Chelsea got back to winning ways by turning on the magic to completely de-feather the Canaries, extending their lead at the top of the Premiership to six points. At the same time, they gave their fans a wonderful pre-Christmas present.

This was the sixth time José's team had scored four goals in a Premiership game in 2004/05, and the final result could well have been 7-0/8-0, even though Chelsea didn't play all that well against a rather poor Norwich team, who were lying sixteenth in the table. Goalkeeper Rob Green produced at least three world-class saves for the visitors.

Chelsea (4-4-2): Cech, Ferreira, Terry, Gallas, Bridge, Lampard, Makélélé, Tiago (Parker), Duff, Robben (Kezman), Gudjohnsen (Drogba).
Norwich (4-4-2): Green, Edworthy, Fleming, Doherty, Charlton, Jonson, Helveg, Safri (McVeigh), Bentley, Huckerby, Svenson (McKenzie).
Attendance: 42,071

Against a rather poor Norwich team, whose defending at times was certainly generous, Chelsea created several chances and although a few were missed, they did succeed in netting some spectacular goals.

Chelsea were three up, and the contest was over before half-time. In-form winger Damien Duff scored an early opener followed up by a Frank Lampard rocket and another special from Dutch hero Arjen Robben.

Despite all their possession and dominance, Chelsea didn't grab a fourth goal until ten minutes from time when substitute Didier Drogba put the icing on the Stamford Bridge cake with a clinical finish.

José knew well in advance that he would need to make a rare enforced change to his now standard Premiership starting line-up. With Ricardo Carvalho absent through injury, William Gallas moved across to play alongside John Terry, allowing Wayne Bridge to return at left back.

Norwich fielded an unchanged team from their last game, a 3-2 home win over Bolton.

Chelsea fashioned very little in the way of attacks early on, but there was no need for concern as Norwich arrived in London bearing a sack full of presents.

As early as the tenth minute, when attempting to play his way out of defence, Thomas Helveg, the former Milan player and Danish international, disastrously rolled the ball to an unmarked Duff. Thank you very much, as the Irishman controlled the ball, moved forward and scored – 1-0. This was the fifth opening goal scored by Duff in nine games.

Chelsea had a strong penalty appeal for handball by substitute Leon McKenzie turned down a few minutes later but, surprisingly, that would be the last scare in the visitors' defence until past the half-hour mark. In fact, 'keeper Rob Green had just two long-range efforts from Lampard fired at him.

José waved his arms around in annoyance as his players, at times, sent wayward passes in all directions ... and you couldn't blame this sloppiness on a new pitch that was throwing up divots over various sections.

At last, Chelsea got back on track when Lampard netted a beauty on thirty-four minutes. Once again, it was a Norwich mistake that led to the goal. A misplaced pass by the lackadaisical Gary Doherty was picked up by Robben. He quickly moved the ball onto Lampard, who found the top-right corner of Green's net from 25 yards with a peach of a shot. This was a truly great strike. Ten minutes later it was 3-0 and game over, as those inside Stamford Bridge witnessed one of the best team goals you could ever wish to see.

The tricky Robben made the first incision, delivering the ball low into the danger-zone for Lampard. The England man knocked it sideways to Portuguese midfielder Tiago, who produced a smart back-heel, to free Robben who finished the move off with a cracking low drive.

It was another beauty. And with the three points assured, thoughts began to turn to what the final score would, and could be, if Chelsea clicked into anything like top gear.

A fourth goal almost arrived four minutes after the break, but Tiago was just an inch or two over with his 18-yard drive. Lampard also volleyed over from Duff's corner. Chelsea couldn't quite hit top form, but Drogba, replacing Gudjohnsen, should have scored when Robben set him free. However, his first touch was too strong and Green saved.

The Norwich 'keeper had the Dutchman at his near post while, soon after, Lampard hit a shot wide after Tiago had robbed the Norwich midfield. Green was forced into action again, saving well from Lampard as Chelsea searched for a fourth goal. At last it arrived when, on eighty-two minutes, a set-piece did the trick.

Claude Makélélé's hopeful shot was diverted away for a corner. Duff took the flag kick and Drogba did what he does best, rising above everyone to power a header into the bottom corner of Green's net.

This was the ninth pre-Christmas game in ten seasons that Chelsea had won. They were top of the Premier League and definitely having a laugh. Who was going to stop them?

Chelsea rounded off the year with further wins over Aston Villa (1-0) and Portsmouth (2-0), before entering 2005 with a single-goal victory at Liverpool, following up by beating Middlesbrough 2-0 at home. The future was certainly looking rosy for José and his men.

CHELSEA 3 SCUNTHORPE UNITED 1
8 January 2005

There could well have been a major shock at Stamford Bridge in this third round encounter as Chelsea – not at their best by a long chalk – edged past their plucky lower League opponents with an adequate performance. This brought José Mourinho his first ever FA Cup victory as a manager.

A BBC reporter stated, 'Chelsea laboured to an unconvincing FA Cup win over Scunthorpe as they overcame the shock of falling behind'. Another indicated that 'José's team simply limped to victory – unable to up their game against resolute opponents', while José himself confirmed: 'We were fortunate to win.'

The 'Iron', managed by Brian Laws, were lying second in Football League Two at the time of kick-off, and had been playing pretty well. They were eager to get a crack at a Premiership club, and they certainly caused Chelsea a few problems as the tie unfolded.

Chelsea (4-4-2): Cudicini, Johnson, Watt, Morais, Smertin, A. Cole, Tiago, Geremi (Ferreira), Gudjohnsen, Kezman (Robben), Drogba (Jarosik).
Scunthorpe (4-5-1): Musselwhite, Byrne, Crosby, Butler, Ridley, Sparrow, Baraclough, Kell, Beagrie (Williams), Hayes, Rankine (Taylor).
Attendance: 40,019

Chelsea, the Premiership leaders, were rocked as early as the fourth minute when Matt Sparrow's low cross found top-scorer Paul Hayes who rolled his marker, Alexei Smertin, inside the penalty area to fire League Two side Scunthorpe into a deserved lead, the ball going through 'keeper Carlo Cudicini's legs. In fact, this goal was only the fourth scored by a visiting team at Stamford Bridge that season.

After some tentative play, and a couple of close shaves at both ends of the pitch, Chelsea, perhaps surprisingly, equalised due to Mateja Kezman's thumping volley at twenty-six minutes. Andy Butler's defensive header fell just right for the Serbian striker, who hit the ball as-sweet-as-you-like past Paul Musselwhite.

Two minutes later, Chelsea's defenders switched off again when, following a corner, Cudicini had to react sharply to claw away Butler's well-timed header.

Chelsea came out for the second half in a more confident and determined mood and, after a spell of pressure, they drew level, albeit with a dose of good fortune when skipper Andy Crosby was unable to avoid the ball as Drogba swept in a low cross.

The underdogs, however, wouldn't lie down. After substitute Cleveland Taylor, a former Bolton Wanderers reserve, had headed against a post, the same player then fired wide from 12 yards with only Cudicini to beat. With Chelsea on the back foot, Crosby missed an even better chance to make amends when Cudicini misjudged Peter Beagrie's cross, but from 3 yards out, the Iron skipper volleyed into the side netting.

With fifteen minutes remaining, Chelsea, who had been under the cosh for quite a while, almost fell behind when Taylor rose to thump a header against the woodwork. This was close, and the luck held for José's team who sealed victory four minutes from time, when Gudjohnsen was on hand to score from close range after Scunthorpe 'keeper Musselwhite fumbled Robben's low shot.

In an interview after the game, José Mourinho said:

I didn't have a very strong defensive line-up. Only Glen Johnson was a regular as a right-back. It was the first game for Scottish centre half Steven Watt, and the first for Russian Alexei Smertin as a centre-back. It was also the first outing for Portuguese U21 international Nuno Morais, who is not a left-back, he's a midfielder. But I'm very happy with their performances.

In response, Scunthorpe boss Brian Laws said:

I was proud of the players and a shade disappointed, as they didn't get anything more out of the game. We had our chances to equalise. Cleveland Taylor had a volley brilliantly saved and he also hit the post. We were pressing them hard, but the third goal killed us. Overall, the players did the town, the fans and the club proud – I could not have asked for any more from them.

In the next round, Chelsea were drawn at home against Birmingham City.

MANCHESTER UNITED 1 CHELSEA 2
(won 2-1 on aggregate)
26 January 2005

After a goalless draw in the first leg at Stamford Bridge, when an irate José alleged that United boss Alex Ferguson influenced the match referee, Chelsea produced a wonderful display in the return game at Old Trafford. They deservedly reached their first League Cup final for seven years, and only their fourth since the competition started in 1960–61.

José, in fact, took a £240 bottle of wine to Old Trafford with him, but it might as well have been a glass of hemlock (Portuguese for poison) he handed to Sir Alex, after his team had clinched victory with Damien Duff's dramatic eighty-fifth minute free-kick.

United (4-1-3-2): Howard, G. Neville, Heinz, Ferdinand, Keane, Silvestre, Ronaldo, Fortune (Rooney), Saha, Scholes, Giggs.
Chelsea (4-4-2): Cech, Ferreira, Terry, Gallas, Bridge, Makélélé, Tiago, Lampard, Robben (J. Cole), Drogba (Gudjohnsen), Duff (Jarosik).
Attendance: 66,885

Before the game, Ferguson had talked about Chelsea wavering in the Premiership if they failed to beat United and reach the final. Was he having a laugh?

This certainly wound up José and his troops in blue, who responded brilliantly, and the boss was duly rewarded for his decision not to keep the normal League Cup goalkeeper, Carlo Cudicini, between the posts, selecting Petr Cech instead. And it was his two terrific saves in the second half that effectively saw Chelsea home. Leaving Wayne Rooney on the bench, and including hard-man Roy Keane, was a way of attaching a certificate of authenticity to the tie.

United, with home advantage, made the better start. Both wide men, Ronaldo and Ryan Giggs, looked threatening, as did Louis Saha who burst in from the left in the nineteenth minute, only to be stopped in his tracks by William Gallas.

After some rather ineffective goalmouth activity, it was Chelsea who struck the first blow on the half hour-mark. Frank Lampard started the move in his own half of the field, and fed Didier Drogba. With right-back Gary Neville preoccupied with watching Drogba, Rio Ferdinand failed to detect any danger as Lampard took

Drogba's return pass in his stride before shooting impeccably across Howard and into the corner of the net. Eight minutes after the goal, Ferguson threw his arms in the air when referee Rob Styles failed to award a penalty after Wayne Bridge, in chesting down John Terry's clearance, fouled Quinton Fortune in the process. Yes, no, don't know!

Taking the lead encourages any side, but its impact on Chelsea was, and still is, particularly significant. United, fighters to the last, powered forward in search of an equaliser but couldn't break through a tightly-packed, and resolute, Chelsea defence.

The passion of the home support reached bedlam after the interval, as the Red Army attacked in force without success. Then, with almost an hour gone, Fergie brought on Rooney in place of Fortune. And with his second touch, the former Everton player found Keane, whose shot from a tight angle flew a yard wide. Soon afterwards, Gallas produced a terrific tackle to stop Rooney moving in on goal.

It was plain to see at this juncture that Chelsea were getting pushed back. In the sixty-third minute, Lampard found space to unleash a stinging drive, which was turned aside by goalkeeper Tim Howard. Shortly afterwards, Drogba's rolled pass across the United area was dummied by Tiago, allowing Arjen Robben to shoot at goal, but his effort was blocked by the right leg of the American goalkeeper.

United eventually equalised in the sixty-eighth minute when Neville hit a high pass downfield to Giggs who had darted between Terry and Gallas. Assessing the situation to perfection, the Welsh international controlled the ball before beating Chelsea's 6ft 5in 'keeper, Cech, with a superbly executed lob.

It was a wonderful goal, and was the first that the Gallas-Terry central defensive partnership had conceded all season. It was now game on and, with almost a third of the match remaining, United knew they had to score again or Chelsea would go through to the final on the away-goal rule.

However, by pushing extra men forward, United left space at the back and Lampard almost scored again for Chelsea. With the home fans roaring them on, Fergie's men became frustrated, and with just five minutes remaining, Damien Duff won the game.

Referee Styles awarded a free-kick close to the right touch-line, some 50 yards from goal. Duff swung the ball into the danger-zone, and with players watching each other (some of them seemingly spellbound), it bounced away from 'keeper Howard and into the far corner of the net. Joy for José and the 2,500 travelling Chelsea supporters ... dismay and heartache for the United fans. Ah well!

Right at the death, Bridge, in the right position at the right time, made a magnificent goalline clearance from a well-directed header by Mikaël Silvestre, while Cech saved superbly from Cristiano Ronaldo.

This was one hell of a forty-second birthday present for José. His Chelsea team had been efficient, totally committed and hugely competent, and would now go on to face Liverpool in the final at Cardiff's Millennium Stadium on 27

February. Could Chelsea win four trophies in one season? The quadruple was still a possibility.

NB: Before this defeat, Manchester United had not been beaten in a domestic semi-final under Sir Alex Ferguson – a record that lasted for nineteen matches.

CF BARCELONA 2 CHELSEA 1
23 February 2005

Chelsea, who had Didier Drogba controversially sent off ten minutes into the second half, battled hard and long and were a shade unlucky to lose by the odd goal in three, at the Camp Nou Stadium in Barcelona. At 1-0 down at interval, the Spanish champions came back to win 2-1, but that away goal was to prove extremely precious for José's men. It was a crying shame that such a terrific game had to be spoilt by a rash and card-happy Swedish referee. Shame on you Anders Frisk!

Barcelona (4-4-2): Valdes, Belletti (Gerard), Marquez, Puyol, Van Bronckhorst, Xavi, Deco, Albertini (Iniesta), Giuly (Maxi Lopez), Ronaldinho, Eto'o.
Chelsea (4-5-1): Cech, Paulo Ferreira, Terry, Carvalho, Gallas, Makélélé, Lampard, Cole (Johnson), Duff (Gudjohnsen), Tiago (Smertin), Drogba.
Attendance: 88,598

Ivorian international, Drogba, was sent packing for an innocuous-looking challenge on goalkeeper Victor Valdes ten minutes into the second half. At the time, Chelsea were leading – and deservedly so – thanks to Juliano Belletti's own-goal just past the half hour mark, when the Barcelona right-back deflected Damien Duff's cross past his 'keeper Valdes.

With a player up, Barça surged forward. Substitute Maxi Lopez fired the Spaniards level on sixty-six minutes, before Samuel Eto'o smashed in the winner with just over fifteen minutes remaining.

It was desperately unlucky for Chelsea, who had looked relatively comfortable until Barcelona were gifted a numerical advantage by the flamboyant Swedish official.

Duff, having been so emphatically excluded by José just twenty-four hours earlier, was a shock inclusion in the starting line-up, and it was the former Blackburn Rovers winger who made the most significant impact for Chelsea in the first half.

Barcelona flew out of the blocks. The usually assured Ronaldinho was uncharacteristically off-target after only two minutes following an error in midfield by Frank Lampard.

The Brazilian looked in a dangerous mood, and soon afterwards he forced Chelsea goalkeeper, Petr Cech, to clutch a dangerous low cross as Barcelona pressed. But Chelsea's resolute defenders soaked up all the pressure that came their way, before delivering a classic counter-punch to take what, to some, was a surprise lead after thirty-two minutes.

Lampard released Duff down the right flank, and with Drogba and Joe Cole unmarked in the centre, waiting for the Irishman's precise cross, Belletti unwittingly turned the ball into his own net as he tried to clear the danger. Two minutes later, Drogba, unmarked, then missed a glorious chance to score a crucial second goal for Chelsea, firing wide with only Valdes to beat after some smart work by the industrious Claude Makélélé. Before the interval, Lampard and Drogba, and Ronaldinho and Samuel Eto'o all had half-chances, but neither were on target with their efforts.

After a tame opening to the second-half, Drogba, who had seen a lot of the ball and had been bustled from pillar to post, was harshly sent off by referee Frisk, following a clash with Valdes in the fifty-fifth minute. The striker had every right to challenge when Belletti's back-pass fell short, but Frisk stunned everyone in the stadium by brandishing the red card as Valdes rolled in agony from the challenge. Nine out of ten for Valdes for artistic impression!

Barcelona made an instant change, sending on Andres Iniesta for Demetrio Albertini, and the midfield substitute almost equalised seven minutes later, firing inches wide with Cech well beaten. Lopez had also entered the fray, and he had been on the pitch for a mere three minutes when he put Barcelona level. Taking a clever pass from Eto'o, he took aim and beat Cech with a comprehensive finish.

With Chelsea back-pedaling, and under pressure for the first time in the match, Ricardo Carvalho and John Terry performed minor miracles as they threw themselves in front of numerous clear shooting chances as José's team clung on desperately.

Unfortunately, their resistance was broken again with seventeen minutes remaining. Lopez found enough room to get in a low shot. To most, he was clearly firing towards the net but, somehow, the ball found its way through to the waiting Eto'o who flashed a first-time finish past Cech.

Chelsea tried in vain to conjure up a second goal, Lampard shooting wide, but it was not to be, and in the end, it was a case of what might have been had not a referee intervened to spoil the contest.

After the match, José who claimed he saw Barcelona head coach Frank Rijkaard meet with referee Frisk during the half-time break, said, 'We were robbed. We didn't deserve to lose. That's it.'

CHELSEA 3 LIVERPOOL 2
(after extra time)
27 February 2005

This five-goal thriller at the Millennium Stadium, Cardiff, was a cracking game of football – quite brilliant.

Kevin McCarra of the Guardian *wrote, 'This final was bigger than the tournament itself. A season that was swirling away from Chelsea is once more sweeping them towards honours. At the end of a week pitted by the defeats to Newcastle United and Barcelona there is the sheen of José Mourinho's first trophy in England, with the League Cup lodged at Stamford Bridge. This was just the performance José had asked for following the 2-1 defeat against Barcelona just four days earlier. No less than fifteen 'overseas-born' players started the final (seven from Chelsea) and five more entered the game as substitutes.*

Chelsea (4-4-2): Cech, Ferreira, Carvalho, Terry, Gallas, (Kezman), Makélélé, Jarosik (Gudjohnsen), Lampard, Drogba, J. Cole (Johnson), Duff.
Liverpool (4-5-1): Dudek, Finnan, Carragher, Hyypia, Traore (Biscan), Hamann, Kewell (Nunez), Gerrard, Garcia, Morientes (Baros), Riise.
Attendance: 77,902

Spectators were still taking their seats when John Arne Riise, playing on the left side of midfield, scored for Liverpool after just forty-five seconds. Fernando Morientes, playing in the seventeenth Cup Final of his professional career, collected a Steven Gerrard pass, turned away from Claude Makélélé on the right and hit a lethal cross towards the far post. The Chelsea defence, including right-back Paulo Ferreira, had bunched in the middle of the penalty area. The ball eluded them all, allowing the unmarked Riise free to smash a volley beyond Petr Cech from the corner of the 6-yard box.

Thankfully, that early goal allowed Chelsea plenty of time to collect themselves, and José's side could even afford to spend half an hour in shock before getting down to business and beating the Merseysiders. However, despite being a goal down, from the thirty-first minute onwards, Chelsea were far superior and held possession with much confidence. This made it even more embarrassing for the Liverpool supporters, who had never before seen their team give the ball away so casually and with such carelessness. The Reds had fleeting moments for sure, but never looked like beating on-form Cech in the Chelsea goal. He was superb, thwarting at least five Liverpool players with consummate ease. In fact, Cech would not have played in the final had Carlo Cudicini, the back-up goalkeeper, not been suspended. Carlo was, however, given the honour of leading out Chelsea.

Liverpool's impressive 'keeper, Jerzy Dudek, was also in good form and pulled off two excellent saves as Chelsea searched for an equaliser. Frank Lampard, who had been going through a muted spell, was an incessant danger with his range of passing. He also had an effort blocked in front of goal with Dudek out of position.

Chances were created and missed, and defenders of both teams, at times, looked rather uncertain when high crosses were delivered into the danger-zone. But both goals survived.

With twenty-nine minutes gone, striker Drogba was sent clear, but saw his weak shot turned aside by Dudek. Ten minutes after the interval, Lampard sent Drogba clear on the left, but Steve Finnan foiled him with an excellent and unexpected challenge.

Liverpool's German midfielder, Didier Hamann, worked a move with Luis Garcia after sixty-four minutes, and shot vigorously from the edge of the area. But Cech had the reflexes and reach to dive to his right and block with a strong hand. This was a crucial save. With time fast running out, and chances few and far between, Chelsea, against the run of play, found themselves level on seventy-nine minutes when Gerrard conceded an own-goal.

Hamann conceded a free-kick that Paulo Ferreira hit across a packed penalty area from the right. Gerrard, leaping in the midst of a group of teammates, got only a glancing touch on the ball with his head, but it was strong enough to see it fly into his own net via the inside of the post.

There is no doubt that the Liverpool skipper, who has so often willed his team to a win, had doomed his club here. Four minutes earlier, he had spurned a great chance to guarantee victory when, from 6 yards, he drove a left-footer wide after a measured cross from the substitute Antonio Nunez.

That shock equaliser scrambled Chelsea's form for a while and Claude Makélélé, who would eventually return to being his relentlessly reliable self, toiled through an error-ridden patch. Nonetheless, it was obvious that Liverpool were struggling to get their game back on track. Lampard's prompting, coupled with the darting runs of Damien Duff and the threat of Didier Drogba through the middle, gave Chelsea the initiative. Riise headed a swerving cross by William Gallas over his own bar and soon afterwards, Dudek, who hurt a knee in a double save from Duff, saved well from Drogba. The Polish goalkeeper also parried a header from Eidur Gudjohnsen, who had come on for Kezman, and also thwarted Gallas from the rebound.

José also introduced Glen Johnson and reverted to having a sedate back four to protect Chelsea's interests. He knew, with Liverpool disconsolate and wearying, that he needed only to wait for victory as the game went into extra time.

Right from the start of the first period of extra time, Chelsea were on the front foot, but their early attacks broke down. Then, in the one-hundred-and-seventh minute, Johnson released a long throw-in from the right that cleared Sami Hyypia at the near post. Drogba, anticipating a mistake by the Liverpool centre-back, pounced to slip the ball home from close range.

Five minutes later, Dudek failed to clear a teasing cross and was stranded as Gudjohnsen turned the ball back for Kezman to knock in his fourth goal of the season. Liverpool responded immediately, and the lively Nunez headed a scrappy second goal from Riise's throw-in with seven minutes remaining. Cech failed to find a route to attack the ball, with conviction, in a crowded penalty area.

Once in the lead, Chelsea – compact in defence and midfield – were never going to let their lead slip, and they held on comfortably to bring José his first trophy in English football. The 'Special One' was not allowed on the pitch at the end after being sent off, apparently for putting his finger to his lips to hush the Liverpool fans. He did, however, celebrate in style with his players afterwards.

CHELSEA 4 CF BARCELONA 2
(won 5-4 on aggregate)
8 March 2005

What a game, what a performance, what a win ... and how José Mourinho and his players celebrated after knocking out one of the competition's favourites, while also scoring four goals against the Spanish giants – a rare achievement in itself.

Chelsea, brilliant early on, looked like crushing Barcelona as they roared into a three-goal lead inside the first twenty minutes. But, in the end, José's men only just squeezed past the post and into the quarter-finals of the Champions League on a great night at Stamford Bridge. In fact, Chelsea were, in truth, on the verge of elimination with fifteen minutes remaining. And there were certainly a few thousand tense and nervous home fans, and certainly a lot of short fingernails.

Chelsea (4-4-2): Cech, Ferreira (Johnson), Terry, Carvalho, Gallas, Makélélé, Lampard, J. Cole, Duff, Kezman, Gudjohnsen (Tiago).
Barcelona (4-4-2): Valdes, Belletti (Giuly), Puyol, Olegguer, Van Bronckhorst (Silvinho), Gerard Lopez, Deco, Xavi, Iniesta (Maxi Lopez), Ronaldinho, Eto'o.
Attendance: 41,315

Let's be truthful, even the most ardent Chelsea supporter, knowing his/her team was trailing 2-1 from the first leg, and missing the suspended Didier Drogba, would have to score four goals to reach the last eight of the Champions League. Even José Mourinho admitted: 'This will need a huge effort from my players ... it's a mighty tough challenge.'

Future Blues' striker Samuel Eto'o's ill-chosen words before the game, when he said that Chelsea 'would record one goal at most and that his own side would therefore go through if they hit the net at all' riled a few. In fact, the Cameroon forward had much to reflect on when, because with just twenty minutes gone, Barcelona were 3-0 down and struggling.

This intensely gripping second leg was certainly as absorbing as the first encounter at the Camp Nou. José chose to include both Mateja Kezman and Eidur Gudjohnsen as his front two. Was it a plan to keep Barcelona's attack at arm's length and strike on the break? Whatever it was, his selection worked a treat, certainly in the opening exchanges.

After just eight minutes, Xavi lost the ball to Frank Lampard, whose deliberate pass down the right was instantly transferred towards the left by Kezman, allowing Gudjohnsen to cut inside Gerard before finding the net with a clinical finish.

With seventeen minutes gone, and Chelsea driving forward, a shot from Joe Cole was deflected towards goal. Barça's goalkeeper, Victor Valdes, at full stretch, could only palm the ball away to Lampard who netted with ease. Two minutes later, Kezman laid the ball back, quite firmly, to Cole, who instantly freed Damien Duff who darted in from the left to slide his low shot past the groping Valdes. Then, perhaps surprisingly to many, Chelsea lost the initiative, and from a position of strength, suddenly started to struggle.

Barcelona started to press, Chelsea dropped deeper, and it was only a super save by Petr Cech, who tipped an Eto'o drive over at twenty-three minutes, that kept the scoreline at 3-0.

Within four minutes, however, Frank Rijkaard's side finally struck – after a questionable penalty decision. There is no doubt whatsoever that right-back Paulo Ferreira did not intend to handle Juliano Belletti's cross, but imposing Italian referee, Pierluigi Collina, felt the Chelsea player's arm had been raised to a rash height. No way! With an irate José looking on, Ronaldinho slid home the penalty.

The Brazilian's next goal, however, needed no assistance ... it was a real beauty.

Seven minutes from half-time, Chelsea defender Ricardo Carvalho failed to get in a decent challenge on Ronaldinho, who used him as a shield to block Cech's view before bending a brilliant 20-yarder into the corner of the net, with the goalkeeper virtually static inside his 6-yard box.

In Barça's next attack, the impressive Ronaldinho released Eto'o, whose effort skimmed the top of the bar. But Chelsea weren't done, and with the whistle ready to sound, Cole struck a post. Phew – this was exciting stuff.

José had intended to have a game like this, and soon after the restart, Lampard almost scored with a header from Duff's corner while, at the other end, Cech was fully extended when saving Belletti's 25-yard drive. Then Carvalho's timely lunge sent the ball behind, with Eto'o ready to outstrip him. At this juncture, Barcelona were looking good, but they knew if Chelsea scored again, they would have it all to do.

The minutes started to tick by. Andrés Iniesta fired against a post in the seventy-fourth minute, and Ronaldinho was only a yard away from connecting with a right-wing cross. With just under fifteen minutes remaining, Chelsea regained the aggregate lead, which they would retain until the last kick.

Duff delivered the perfect corner, allowing Chelsea's centre-back, John Terry, to jump and turn to glide the ball into the net past a startled Valdes. The ground suddenly erupted. Chelsea were 4-2 in front on the night, 5-4 overall.

After that, Chelsea's defenders were not unduly troubled. Barça's fire was slowly fading out. There was no way back for the Spaniards, and when given the chance, the old campaigners in blue kept possession. They did the simple things and played out time to record a famous victory.

This was a game so intoxicating that heads were still spinning almost a decade later.

CHELSEA 4 BAYERN MUNICH 2
5 April 2005

Having scored four goals against Barcelona a month earlier, Chelsea rattled in another four against the German champions, Bayern Munich. How many teams have done that?

With the Carling Cup and the Premiership title already safely in the bag, Chelsea were smack bang on course to win the Champions League as well. However, the bookies were reasonably confident that José's men could, even would, triumph, by offering decent odds of 3-1, some even going to 7-2.

Bayern went into this quarter-final first-leg encounter minus the injured duo of Claudio Pizarro and Roy Makaay, who had already netted forty goals between them during the season. With this in mind, Chelsea Blues certainly fancied their chances against the Germans.

Chelsea (4-4-2): Cech, Johnson (Huth), Terry, Carvalho, Gallas, Makélélé, J. Cole (Tiago), Lampard, Drogba (Forssell), Gudjohnsen, Duff.
Bayern Munich (4-5-1): Kahn, Sagnol, Lizarazu, Frings, Lucio, Kovak, Salihamidzic (Schweinsteiger), Ballack, Guerrero, Ze Roberto (Scholl), Hargreaves.
Attendance: 40,253

Having been banned from the touchline after the episode with referee Anders Frisk in the Barcelona game in February, José exiled himself entirely after liaising with his coaching staff and assistants. José agreed to field a 4-2-1-3 formation, with Damien Duff, Joe Cole and Didier Drogba up front, and Eidur Gudjohnsen as an attacking midfielder. Was this brave, brilliant or foolhardy? The 'Special One' knew what he was doing, and it worked a treat. Top man.

Chelsea's defence had managed to keep only one clean sheet in their previous nine fixtures before taking on the German side, and right at the start, Cech was in action.

However, it was Chelsea who struck the first blow. In the fourth minute, Robert Kovac was put under pressure by Didier Drogba's challenge for a high ball. His poor header was collected by Duff, who set up Joe Cole for a drive, which would surely have been saved by Oliver Kahn, but a deflection off of centre-back, Lucio, took the ball past him and into the net.

Unduly worried, Bayern hit back immediately and gained midfield supremacy for an extended period. Chelsea, although a goal up, seemed hesitant, conceding two quick free-kicks on the edge of their penalty area, which Owen Hargreaves and Ze Roberto wasted. José's men simply couldn't get hold of the ball, and this was the case for the majority of the first half, which saw Bayern have seventy per cent of the play, yet Petr Cech was very rarely troubled.

Chelsea began the second half much more positively. When Drogba played the ball in, Eidur Gudjohnsen fed Duff, but the Irishman's direct shot was saved by Kahn. Bayern then got going again, and when William Gallas brought down substitute Bastian Schweinsteiger after fifty-two minutes, the resulting free-kick struck the defensive wall, and from the rebound, Ze Roberto saw his shot pushed away by the diving figure of Cech. It only reached as far as Schweinsteiger, who cracked the loose ball low into the net. The score was now 1-1 – game on.

As it happened, it was Chelsea who reacted to being pegged rather than the Germans on drawing level, and at this point, Frank Lampard began to display all the qualities of a world-class footballer. At fifty-nine minutes, Drogba, despite having two defenders close to him, climbed highest to knock down a long ball from Glen Johnson. Lampard, moving in for the kill, connected powerfully with his left foot to drive it low into the corner of the net past Kahn whose vision, it seemed, was slightly obscured by the presence of Lucio in front of him.

It was all Chelsea now, and eleven minutes later, with Bayern looking shell-shocked, Duff's attempted pass deflected to Claude Makélélé who chipped a shot cross back into the danger area where Lampard, showing remarkable technique, spun round and took the ball on his chest, before firing another left-footer beyond the despairing dive of 'keeper Kahn.

Two close shaves followed, as Bayern came under more pressure. In the eighty-first minute, the visitors fell further behind. Their defence was at sixes and sevens following Lampard's corner and, although Gudjohnsen couldn't convert the initial half-chance, Drogba was on hand to ram the loose ball past Kahn from close range.

At 4-1 up, with less than ten minutes remaining, Chelsea were on cloud nine. So too was a delighted José – somewhere in the ground.

Bayern, to their credit, gave it one last flourish and one minute into added time, they were awarded a controversial penalty for handball against the unlucky Ricardo Carvalho. Everyone inside Stamford Bridge – and millions more watching on TV – knew that future Chelsea man, Michael Ballack, would convert from the spot – and he did. The goal clearly revived a Champions League quarter-final, which José's team appeared to have killed stone dead. Some say that had Makaay been fit to play, it would have been a different kettle of fish, with Bayern calling the shots and scoring the goals. We will never know.

After this win, José signed an improved contract with Chelsea that would see him paid £5.2 million a year, until the end of the deal in 2008.

BAYERN MUNICH 3 CHELSEA 2
(Chelsea won 6-5 on aggregate)
12 April 2005

Having gained a two-goal advantage in their first leg at Stamford Bridge, Chelsea knew they had to score in Germany. It was imperative, simply because Bayern, around this time, rarely failed to find the net when playing on their home patch in Munich. José Mourinho was well aware of this and started the game with four centre-backs, preferring Robert Huth at right-back in the place of Glen Johnson, as Paulo Ferreira was still out injured. He also chose two attacking midfielders, two strikers and a winger. He selected a pretty strong bench as well, from which to choose three substitutes.

Bayern included former Chelsea midfielder, Michael Ballack, in their line-up and, before kick-off, his boss, Felix McGath, talked about Lampard being the key player (remember he had scored twice in the first leg). McGath said, 'I know Lampard can score goals; he always will, so we need to defend well and then the Lampard problem will not be there.'

Bayern Munich (4-4-2): Kahn, Sagnol, Lizarazu (Salihamidzic), Demichilis (Scholl), Lucio, Kovac, Schweinsteiger, Ballack, Makaay (Guerrero), Pizarro, Ze Roberto.
Chelsea (4-3-1-2): Cech, Huth, Terry, Carvalho, Gallas, Makélélé, J. Cole (Nuno Morias), Lampard, Drogba, Gudjohnsen (Geremi), Duff (Tiago).
Attendance: 58,719

This was an excellent game of football and a superb result for Chelsea. José Mourinho did everything right on the night and he was a very proud man at the final whistle.

It came as no surprise to see Bayern fly out of the traps, but their early attacks were wasteful and Chelsea's sole defence dealt comfortably with everything the Germans threw at them. In fact, Chelsea had the first chance, but Drogba failed to get any pace on his shot from 12 yards, and Oliver Kahn smothered his effort while Ballack's shot was blocked by Terry. Cech saved low down from Ze Roberto.

After a certain amount of cat and mouse, it was Frank Lampard, assisted by a ricochet, who put Chelsea ahead after half an hour to stun the home crowd. Joe Cole shook off Schweinsteiger as he drifted in from the left before rolling the ball to an unmarked Lampard some 25 yards from goal. Chelsea's top-scorer moved forward, took aim and struck a sweet low shot that flicked off Lucio's heel and completely wrong-footed Oliver Kahn. It was 1-0 to the Blues, who now led 5-2 overall.

The thousands of disgruntled spectators inside the Allianz Arena were shell-shocked, as were some of the Bayern players, and for the next fifteen minutes they couldn't string two passes together. Nerves had set in, and Chelsea were in total command.

Bayern's frustrated boss, McGath, made an early second-half change, bringing on Mehmet Scholl for Demichilis, but his first bit of action saw him commit a foul on Lampard. At 1-0 down, Bayern required three unanswered goals to advance. But Chelsea still had notions of adding to their lead, and with almost an hour on the clock, Drogba occupied the two centre-backs at a free-kick, allowing Duff to dash through a gap, only to be frustrated by Kahn's fine save.

In the sixty-fifth minute, Bayern equalised. Cech palmed Ballack's downward header against a post, but Pizarro, who had come back from an offside position, knocked in the rebound. Chelsea's protests fell on deaf ears. Five minutes later, a Bixente Lizarazu cross bounced off Huth and hit the bar. Within moments, another Ballack header was booted off the line by no other than Eidur Gudjohnsen.

With Bayern pushing men forward, Chelsea counter-attacked superbly and, in the eightieth minute, Drogba re-established his side's three-goal lead and sewed up the game. Cleverly evading Robert Kovac, Drogba moved forward to head home a Joe Cole cross with venom. With John Terry seemingly struggling with a leg injury and his teammates relaxing – to José's annoyance – Bayern came back to gain an improbable win.

In stoppage time, Paulo Guerrero, substitute, turned in a Bastian Schweinsteiger shot from close range before Scholl was on hand to find the net from a cut-back.

Those last two goals gave Bayern an undeserved 3-2 victory, and for the record, they went unwatched by at least 30,000 home supporters who had already stomped their way to the exits in sheer disgust.

José reminded everyone after the game that more tough opposition would lie ahead, saying, 'We will assess the situation in due course. In the meantime let's go out and win the League.'

BOLTON WANDERERS 0 CHELSEA 2
30 April 2005

Chelsea travelled 200 miles or so north to Bolton, knowing that victory would see them clinch their first League title in fifty years. But they also knew – via the fans, various websites and club stats – that their overall record against the Lancashire club wasn't all that good. Indeed, they had won only two of their previous sixteen League games on Wanderers' soil, at Burnden Park and the Reebok.

Nevertheless, undefeated in twenty-five Premiership games under José Mourinho, Chelsea were full of confidence ahead of what was, effectively, their biggest League game for half a century.

Bolton (5-3-2): Jaaskelainen, Candela (Jaidi), Hierro, N'Gotty, Ben Haim, Gardner, Speed, Giannakopoulos (Pedersen), Okocha, Davies, Diouf (Nolan).
Chelsea (4-4-2): Cech, Geremi, Terry, Carvalho, Gallas, Makélélé (Smertin), Tiago, Lampard, Jarosik, Drogba (Huth), Gudjohnsen (J. Cole).
Attendance: 27,653

Paul Wilson's opening line of his report in the *Guardian* read as follows: 'The wait is over, Chelsea are champions and if there is any justice in the world Frank Lampard's two-goal contribution will secure him the Footballer of the Year award as well!' For sure 'Lamps' was certainly the player of the match at Bolton, his class and commitment shining out like a beacon.

José Mourinho always said he wanted to win the title in Bolton, and by sheer coincidence that's what happened – amazing. Following on from their 3-1 victory over Fulham the previous Saturday, Chelsea were right up for this one – there was no doubting this.

José played two up front – Didier Drogba and Eidur Gudjohnsen – although perhaps ominously for the vital Champions League tie against Liverpool in four days time, wingers Damien Duff and Arjen Robben were rested with minor strains.

Bolton, sixth in the table and blessed with rugged defence, were in no mood to be bridesmaids in their own backyard, especially after taking a point off Chelsea at Stamford Bridge in November. Indeed, Sam Allardyce's team still had hope of a fourth-place finish, which would guarantee them a place in Europe.

After just three minutes, Chelsea 'keeper, Petr Cech, had a deal with a close-range shot from Stelios Giannakopoulos, and soon afterwards, he was in action again as crosses came in from both flanks. In fact, the Czech Republic international continued to be extended throughout the first half, with two unconvincing punches not to his forté. He did, however, save a good header from Gary Speed and a sweetly struck shot from Fernando Hierro, both of which were on target.

Chelsea, it must be said, did not play at all well during the opening forty-five minutes and could easily have gone in at the break, one goal down. Kevin Davies, escaping his markers, met Bruno N'Gotty's well flighted free-kick, but from six yards, his effort lacked power and direction, allowing Cech to make a straightforward save. Chelsea's only threats on the Bolton goal were two speculative efforts from Jiri Jarosik, both of which were way off-target.

José's side simply couldn't get going, and it was plain to see that the absence of the mercurial midfield trio of Duff, Joe Cole and Robben was a key factor.

Lampard and Tiago were being made to cover far too much ground, being pushed back nearer their defence than José wanted.

John Terry, who was caught by Davies' elbow in the first period, was finding it difficult to see out of a swollen eye, but the England defender was first out onto the pitch after the interval, sleeves rolled up and ready for action.

Inspired by their captain's example, Chelsea began to play with a lot more determination and purpose. Bolton were kept at arm's length, and with Terry and Lampard moving the ball through midfield and José urging his players on from his technical area, the visitors began to impose themselves.

Drogba, who at one point was more concerned about a tear in his shorts than terrorising the Bolton defence, started to throw his weight around, and it was the Ivorian striker who was responsible for winning a header that started the move which brought the crucial breakthrough goal in the sixtieth minute.

Drogba's astute flick found Gudjohnsen in space. The Icelander quickly fed Lampard, who cut inside Vincent Candela and, resisting a blatant tug of his shirt, strode into the penalty area before firing the ball past 'keeper Jussi Jaaskelainen. Sheer delight, joy and relief all around as the players, the bench and supporters celebrated.

Bolton boss, Allardyce, wasn't too happy about the goal, which he put down to sloppy and casual defending. And when Chelsea added a decisive second with nine minutes remaining, he was livid. The Whites committed the cardinal error of sending too many men forward for a corner. They paid the price big time.

The ball was cleared out of the danger-zone. Claude Makélélé collected it and steered a smart pass through to Lampard, who calmly carried it forward, through a non-existent defence, rounded Jaaskelainen and scored his second of the game and his eighteenth of the season. This was a great individual goal and it clinched the title.

In between the two goals, Chelsea came close to scoring on three more occasions, whereas Bolton managed just one worthwhile attack. Once the blues had taken the lead, no one was going to breach the meanest defence in the land. In fact, when the final whistle was sounded at the end of their thirty-eighth and final Premiership game of the season, Chelsea's defence had conceded just fifteen goals; six at home, nine away.

A delighted and smiling José said at the after-match press conference, 'Frank [Lampard] has made a habit of getting forward and scoring goals all season. Now he has two extremely memorable ones to treasure.' Next up for the men in blue ... a crucial Champions League semi-final first leg against Liverpool at Stamford Bridge.

CHELSEA 0 LIVERPOOL 1
(Chelsea lost 0-1 on aggregate)
3 May 2005

After a goalless draw in the first leg in front of 40,497 fans at Stamford Bridge, this all-Premiership Champions League semi-final hung in the balance when the teams met for a second time at Anfield.

On their own patch, Didier Drogba and Frank Lampard both missed clear chances for Chelsea in the first half, as José's side pressed for a crucial advantage, while 'keeper Petr Cech saved from John Arne Riise and Milan Baros to deny Liverpool a vital away goal.

The second half was a rather sterile affair, as neither side was able to carve out a clear cut chance. Obviously Liverpool were the far happier of the two sides, and for the return leg on Merseyside, Reds' boss, Rafael Benitez, sent out his predicted side with Czech striker, Milan Baros, leading the attack with the tall German, Dietmar Hamann, making his first start in six weeks, replacing the suspended Xabi Alonso in midfield.

Chelsea's chief was forced to leave his influential Dutchman Arjen Robben on the bench (it was said he was not fully fit following an ankle injury) and unfortunately another wide player, Damien Duff, was ruled out with a tedious hamstring problem, while Geremi was preferred to Glen Johnson in the right-back position.

Liverpool (4-4-2): Dudek Finnan, Carragher, Hyypia, Traore, Garcia (Nunez), Hamann (Kewell), Gerrard, Biscan, Riise, Baros (Cisse).
Chelsea (4-4-2): Cech Geremi (Huth), Carvalho, Terry, Gallas; Tiago (Kezman), Makélélé, Lampard; Cole (Robben), Drogba, Gudjohnsen.
Attendance: 42,529

This tight, evenly matched contest was decided by a controversial goal, scored as early as the fourth minute by Liverpool's Luis García. There was, and still as, huge doubt as to whether García's shot actually crossed the line. The incident itself, though, could have had even more devastating consequences for Chelsea if referee Lubos Michel had interpreted the incident and build up differently. He let play continue after Chelsea's goalkeeper, Petr Cech, had certainly fouled Milan Baros before

Garcia appeared on the scene to roll the ball agonisingly over the line as William Gallas desperately tried to clear his effort to safety.

Liverpool manager, Rafael Benitez, said; 'If we hadn't scored, maybe we would have got a penalty and the Chelsea goalkeeper, shown a red card.'

The goal came when John Arne Riise broke clear down the left. Steven Gerrard gained possession and quickly fed Milan Baros, who lobbed Cech before being fouled by the charging goalkeeper. As the ball broke free, García was on hand to apply the finishing touch – just.

Thereafter, the game wasn't great. There were very few chances at either end, and in fact, the best of the lot came later on, two of them for Chelsea. First, Didier Drogba failed to convert with a seemingly free header in the eighty-third minute, and Icelandic striker Eidur Gudjohnsen flashed a reckless shot wide in the sixth minute of stoppage time.

Substitute Djibril Cissé had Liverpool's best effort, but Cech saved low down. Prior to that, in the sixty-seventh minute, Lampard saw his 30-yard free-kick well saved by Jerzy Dudek, who dived to his right to divert the ball away for a corner. This wasn't a chance, it was a terrific shot that produced a quite wonderful save.

During a rather scrappy first half, Lampard set Joe Cole free, but his low cross found its way straight through Liverpool's 6-yard box as every other Chelsea player failed to read the situation. Two minutes later, Lampard ran into trouble on the edge of his own penalty area and almost presented Hamann with a scoring chance. Just past the half-hour mark, Drogba was far too casual when he had a decent chance to shoot at goal, but allowed his marker to get in a challenge.

Chelsea, it must be said, played well below par, although Drogba did, as usual, turn himself around, without really causing the home defence too much grief. The absence of both Robben (who did come on as a sixty-eighth minute substitute) and Duff proved crucial.

Things improved slightly after the interval, and although chances were few and far between, Chelsea didn't really perform. They lacked the cutting edge to slice through a well-drilled Liverpool defence, and without doubt the clinical, jinking, teasing runs of Robben were sorely missed. As a result, José Mourinho suffered a knockout blow in a major European tournament for the first time in his career.

He said, without a smile on his face,

> The loss of Robben and Duff was the difference between the two teams ... and the best team lost. My players fought and fought and fought. Of course, we are disappointed that we lost, but I am very proud of my players.

For the record, Liverpool, in their fifth European Cup/Champions League final, beat AC Milan on penalties after being 3-0 down at half-time.

THE FA COMMUNITY SHIELD
ARSENAL 1 CHELSEA 2
7 August 2005

Fielding new signing Asier Del Horno from Athletic Bilbao, and naming the returning Hernan Crespo from his loan spell with AC Milan and winger Shaun Wright-Phillips – who had been recruited from Manchester City – on the bench, Chelsea and José got their new season off to a winning start by lifting yet another trophy. This time, it was the FA/Community Shield that found its way to Stamford Bridge for only the third time in the club's history. The two previous wins came in 1955 and 2000.

It wasn't easy against their London rivals, Arsenal, who matched them pass-for-pass, kick-for-kick and tackle-for-tackle, in a tight, if not thrilling, contest at Cardiff's Millennium Stadium. In the end, it was Didier Drogba's two goals that did the trick.

Arsenal started the game with ten foreigners in their line-up, and as the game progressed, introduced another five. Left-back and future Chelsea star, Ashley Cole, was the odd man out. Chelsea fielded eight overseas players and brought on another three, making it twenty-six overseas players in all.

Arsenal (4-4-2): Lehman, Lauren (Hoyte), Toure, Senderos (Cygan), Cole, Flamini (Hleb), Ljungberg (Reyes), Fabregas, Henry, Bergkamp (Van Persie), Pires (Silva). **Chelsea** (4-3-3): Cech, Ferreira, Del Horno, Terry, Gallas, Makélélé, Lampard (Geremi), Duff (J. Cole), Drogba (Crespo), Gudjohnsen (Tiago), Robben (Wright-Phillips).
Attendance: 58,014

Drogba's brace came in the eighth and fifty-seventh minutes. Firstly, the strong, forceful Ivory Coast striker brought down Asier Del Horno's long pass on his chest, before clipping a sweetly-struck volley past Jens Lehman to open the scoring. Then, in Chelsea's fourth attack of the second half, using his powerful frame, he shrugged off challenges from centre half, Philippe Senderos, and Cameroon full back, Lauren, and also 'keeper Lehmann, before guiding a rising shot into the Gunners' net.

Spanish midfielder, Cesc Fabregas, quickly pulled a goal back for Arsenal, sliding the ball past Petr Cech in the sixty-fifth minute after Freddie Ljungberg had crossed hard and low into the penalty area from the right flank.

A BBC reporter wrote, twenty-four hours after the match,

> A new season might have arrived, but on the evidence of Sunday's game, it could be a case of same old story for Premiership holders Chelsea. Last season, José Mourinho's side had the meanest goals against record in the Premiership and, for long periods, Chelsea's defensive blanket smothered Arsenal's attack.

The chief smotherer of the park was workaholic Claude Makélélé, who broke up a succession of Arsenal attacks. Goalkeeper Petr Cech had a typically solid game, his best save coming from Kolo Toure, which saw him push the central defender's shot past the post. That effort by the Arsenal player was in fact, the best the FA Cup holders could manage during the opening half, and this clearly summed up the Gunners' deficiencies as Thierry Henry seemed to produce his best work out on the flanks, causing no danger whatsoever.

As for Chelsea's attack, José was, and is, far better-off with Crespo, Drogba, Gudjohnsen and Robben all capable of scoring at least a dozen or so goals per season. Following his £24 million move from French club, Olympique Marseille, Drogba had a difficult initiation into English football when he netted only ten Premiership goals. In fact, during the summer he had complained to José, in the nicest way possible, saying that he 'demanded too much from him in terms of defensive work.'

Something must surely have been said – both ways – because at the final whistle, both Drogba and his manager were very happy chappies. The two teams renewed their rivalry a fortnight later in the Premiership, when Arsenal travelled to Stamford Bridge. Once again, it was Drogba who stole the headlines, netting the only goal of the game in the seventy-third minute.

CHELSEA 4 WEST BROMWICH ALBION 0
24 August 2005

This was one of the most one-sided games seen at Stamford Bridge for many years. Let's be truthful, Albion, managed by Bryan Robson, were a joke. They failed to get a single effort on target all evening. Chelsea had 70 per cent of the play, and in fact, José's men let the Baggies off far too lightly.

Chelsea (4-5-1): Cudicini, Johnson, Terry, Gallas, Del Horno, Essien, Makélélé, Lampard, J. Cole (Robben), Drogba (Crespo), Wright-Phillips (Duff).
Albion (4-4-2): Kirkland, Albrechtsen, Gaardsoe, Clement, Robinson, Scimeca, Chaplow, Johnson (Inamoto), Greening (Ellington), Kanu, Kamara.
Attendance: 41,201

Albion fielded a much-changed team from that which had beaten Portsmouth 2-1 four days earlier, while José put out what he believed was his best eleven for the occasion, giving home debuts to around £46.5 million worth of talent in midfielder Michael Essien, wide man Shaun Wright-Phillips, and Spanish defender, Asier Del Horno.Chelsea, surprisingly, made a slow start to the game as the torrential rain eventually stopped falling in West London. They were 'slipshod' wrote one reporter, but Albion never threatened either.

Del Horno finally set up a chance for Didier Drogba on twenty-one minutes, but he headed wide of Chris Kirkland's far post. That was a warning for the visitors, and two minutes later, Baggies' central-back, Thomas Gaardsoe, made a grievous error with a poor pass sidewards to his co-defender and ex-Chelsea man, Neil Clement. In came the alert Wright-Phillips, who sent Drogba clear down the right. The Ivory Coast striker's cross, hit low and hard into the danger-zone, was dummied by Essien, leaving either Joe Cole or Lampard free to score. It was the latter who duly obliged, firing home to celebrate the birth of his baby daughter.

After surviving three more close shaves and two near misses, Albion's defence collapsed again two minutes before half-time. Left-back Paul Robinson misjudged the bounce of the ball as Lampard passed to Wright-Phillips. The ball, in fact, seemed to be running over the bye-line, but the former Manchester City man gave chase and pulled it back across goal for Cole to sweep it into the net from 15 yards. Albion's defence was nowhere to be seen.

After another slow start to the second half, Chelsea clicked into overdrive and went three-up at sixty-eight minutes. Once again, Baggies' full-back, Robinson, was initially at fault. Misjudging a pass inside him aimed for Drogba, the ball eluded him and was collected by Essien, whose shot flew off Ricci Scimea's head and out for a corner. The initial flag-kick was cleared, but another followed straightaway. After Robinson had conceded a third, all within a minute, Del Horno's shot across goal was turned in at the far post by the unmarked Drogba.

The impressive and hardworking Cole, who had given Robinson a real runaround all evening, was replaced by substitute Arjen Robben when the game restarted. The Dutchman soon laid on Chelsea's fourth goal with ten minutes remaining. It was an untidy affair inasmuch that Robben's cross bounced off three Albion players inside the penalty-area before Martin Albrechtsen's clearance cannoned off the flying Dutchman and into the path of Lampard, who volleyed the ball home from 10 yards.

There was still time for Kirkland to make a splendid save from Essien's excellent 25-yard drive but, by this time, Albion, utterly bereft of ideas, looking clueless and tired, were completely shot.

After the game, Albion's manager Bryan Robson was criticised by the UEFA President, Sepp Blatter, for deliberately putting out a weak side against Chelsea because the result was a foregone conclusion. The club denied the charge. One livid Baggies' supporter said, 'It's cost me almost £100 to come down to London to watch this rubbish.'

CF BARCELONA 1 CHELSEA 1
(Chelsea lost 2-3 on aggregate)
7 March 2006

José Mourinho knew it would take 'one hell of a performance' by his team to knock Barcelona out of the Champions League. Having lost the first leg 2-1 at Stamford Bridge, Chelsea had to score at least twice at the Camp Nou to stand any chance of reaching the second round. Unfortunately, it was a bridge too far, and although the Blues battled hard and long to earn a creditable 1-1 draw on the night, they fell short, going down by the odd goal of five over the two legs.

CF Barcelona (4-4-2): Valdes, Oleguer, Puyol, Marquez, Van Bronckhorst, Deco, Edmilson, Motta, Messi (Larsson), Ronaldinho, Eto'o.
Chelsea (4-4-2): Cech, Paulo Ferreira, Carvalho, Terry, Gallas, J. Cole (Huth), Makélélé, Lampard, Duff (Gudjohnsen), Robben, Drogba (Crespo).
Attendance: 97,442

Kevin McCarra of the *Guardian* wrote, 'It was a quiet death. With a 3-2 aggregate loss, Chelsea's Champions League campaign passed away in relative tranquility at the Camp Nou.' The honest truth was that Barcelona were far too good for José's men on the night. It was certainly a disappointing result, considering the high standards set by José since his arrival at Stamford Bridge. The simple fact is that Chelsea didn't perform.

The manager's analytical mind clearly told him that there was something amiss in his team and in his philosophy. 'We'll sort it out' he said, 'This is only a hiccup.'

Barcelona, despite losing Lionel Messi early on with an Achilles tendon injury, played well. Ronaldinho was outstanding, and he gave Chelsea's defence a tough time throughout the ninety minutes.

Despite fielding an attack-minded line-up comprised of two wingers, Joe Cole and Damien Duff, and Arjen Robben operating just behind Didier Drogba, Chelsea simply couldn't get going.

Barcelona dominated possession for long periods, but never really troubled Petr Cech. In fact, home 'keeper, Victor Valdes, also had a quiet first half, yet he did produce a fine save to deny Robben in the thirty-eighth minute.

Cech was scarcely beleaguered, yet Barcelona had no incentive to mount an onslaught on his goal. They merely retained the ball, passing it from side to side, backwards and forwards across the field, covering an area of 40–50 yards. It was pretty to watch, but rather boring.

Chelsea could not interrupt Barcelona's pattern of play often enough, although José's tactical plan was understandable as he chose to sacrifice Lampard's adventurous instincts by asking him to help Claude Makélélé as a defensive midfielder.

The home crowd had nothing to worry about. Barcelona always looked in control. Chelsea were virtually second best from the start, although Drogba might have changed this in the ninth minute when, from Joe Cole's cross, he failed to connect with his head. Two minutes from the interval, Paulo Ferreira's free-kick was headed down by Terry to Cole, whose relaxed flick took the ball over both Valdes and the crossbar.

In between times, Cech punched away a dangerous cross from Ronaldinho, Ricardo Carvalho reacted well to block a shot by Thiago Motta, and Samuel Eto'o shot wide. The onus was on Chelsea, and certainly José, to make Barcelona uneasy. It didn't happen.

Frank Rijkaard's back four were coping pretty well, and with his team straining for transformation, José sent on Eidur Gudjohnsen and Hernan Crespo as he switched to a 4-4-2 system, but there was an immediate reaction from Barcelona, Cech blocking a drive from Eto'o. At the other end of the field, Crespo, with his first touch in the sixty-third minute, could only jab a smart Cole pass behind the frame of the goal.

Service of that sort was never sighted again, and with twelve minutes remaining, the Camp Nou crowd celebrated victory when Barcelona substitute, Henrik Larsson, and Eto'o linked up to send Ronaldinho charging past a falling Terry to fire beyond Cech.

To their credit, Chelsea responded – as all Mourinho's teams do – and surprisingly grabbed an equaliser in stoppage time when Giovanni van Bronckhorst was judged, by referee Markus Merk of Germany, to have brought down Terry inside the box. Lampard stepped up to fire home the penalty.

In any other circumstances, a 1-1 draw at the Camp Nou would be a wonderful result. Unfortunately on this occasion it was a poor one for Chelsea. Barcelona went on to beat Chelsea's London rivals, Arsenal, 2-1 in the final in Paris.

BOLTON WANDERERS 0 CHELSEA 2
15 April 2006

Virtually twelve months after winning their first League title for fifty years, it was a case of déjà vu for José Mourinho and Chelsea, who once again defeated Bolton Wanderers to move within four points of retaining the Premiership trophy, with an identical scoreline at the very same venue, in front of a similar crowd. Frank Lampard scored his nineteenth goal of the season, but who scored Chelsea's opener? To this day, the debate still goes on as to whether it was Didier Drogba or John Terry.

Bolton (4-4-2): Jaaskelainen, Ben Haim, N'Gotty, Faye, Gardner, Davies, Nolan, Campo, Speed (Nakata), Vaz Te (Stelios); Borgetti (Pedersen).
Chelsea (4-4-2): Cech, Gérémi, Gallas, Terry, Del Horno, Makélélé; Essien, J. Cole (Ferreira), Lampard, Crespo (Robben), Drogba (Huth).
Attendance: 27,266

Joe Cole was brought into the side by José for the suspended loanee Oliviera Maniche, from Moscow Dynamo, who had been sent off in Chelsea's 4-1 win over West Ham six days earlier.

Chelsea, who had won only one game in the last seven away, started tentatively against a lively Wanderers side, and conceded three free-kicks in their own half inside the first four minutes – two by Del Horno. This didn't please José. Bolton's first long throw almost produced a goal. Cech came for it, changed his mind and slipped, but Gérémi was alert to block Vaz Te's shot.

Crespo was a fraction under a cross on twenty minutes as Chelsea responded. They had a lucky escape a minute later when Vaz Te played a one-two with Borgetti, only to scuff his shot against the post as Cech advanced.

With the home crowd giving Drogba a hard time after he had twice gone down, once winning a free-kick, they turned their attention on Essien on the half-hour, as he lay injured following a challenge by Gardner, who was booked by referee Dowd.

As the game wore on, the quality of football decreased somewhat, although Nolan did flash a shot just over Cech's bar from 25 yards. Crespo was robbed of a certain goal by Gardner's flying header, and Lampard shot straight at Jaaskelainen.

The most overworked performer was certainly referee Phil Dowd, who awarded seventeen fouls, ten against Chelsea, in the first forty minutes. However, he booked only one player, Makélélé, who had been the subject of several of his blows. And when Bolton's Campo was not yellow-carded, a furious José made his feelings known over Dowd's inconsistency. However, José's anger turned to delight when, from Lampard's subsequent forty-fourth minute free-kick, Drogba and Terry rose together. Both seemed to get their head to the ball to send it past Jaaskelainen, which gave Chelsea the lead.

TV replays failed to decipher who the scorer was. Terry said it was his, but a freeze-frame suggested the ball may have hit Drogba's head. Who cared – it was 1-0 to Chelsea.

Chelsea still lacked urgency during the early stages of the second half, and after Cole had committed another silly foul, the midfield went to sleep, allowing Stelios to get away. Del Horno missed his clearance but, thankfully, Pedersen shot over from Ben Haim's cross. Chelsea, struggling to get any width to their attacks, scored a second goal completely out of the blue, to seal the points in the fifty-eighth minute.

Essien won a 50-50 challenge, and sent Crespo scampering up the left with Lampard in support. The midfielder collected the pass, nudged the ball forward before netting his fifteenth Premiership goal of the season, his nineteenth in all competitions, to equal his 2004–05 tally.

At this juncture, the Chelsea fans decided it was time to remember the old guard and chanted the names of Zola, Osgood and Wise. Drogba, not at his best, then lost Faye. But as he turned, he was clearly held back in the area. His claims for a penalty fell on deaf ears.

With thirteen minutes left, Robben missed a golden chance to extend Chelsea's lead. Drogba robbed Gardner and crossed early, but Jaaskelainen slipped Robben's first touch, which let him down.

With eighty minutes gone, Drogba was booked for arguing over a handball incident inside Bolton's penalty area – a ridiculous decision from a referee who had a poor, very poor, game.

Ferreira and Huth came on as late substitutes to bolster up José's defence, and after Huth had been booked for a foul, Campo's tame effort was easily collected by Cech. Bolton's rugged defender Ben Haim tripped Essien in stoppage time and was sent off.

This was a poor game, but a great result for Chelsea. Referee Dowd's final foul count was 38-19 committed by each team, while the bookings favoured Bolton 4-3, plus one red card.

Fact: Ironically, in December 1954, two Leicester City players, George Milburn and Jack Froggatt, were credited with a joint own-goal as Chelsea won 3-1 on their way towards their first-ever League Championship. This joint effort at Bolton set them on their way to a third title.

CHELSEA 1 LIVERPOOL 2
22 April 2006

José Mourinho admitted that he got his 'tactics all wrong', after Liverpool ended Chelsea's hopes of a domestic double with a narrow victory at Old Trafford in the FA Cup semi-final.

Although he knew his plan didn't work on the pitch as he would have liked, the 'Special One' was certainly not impressed when two good chances went begging, both missed by Didier Drogba, before John Arne Riise's free-kick put Liverpool in front.

Looking somewhat disconsolate, he said after the game, 'You have to take those sort of chances in a game like this and we missed one in each half. It means we miss out on a big match and that hurts.'

Starting with only two home-grown players – Terry and Lampard – against Liverpool's four, Chelsea never really produced the form everyone knew they were capable of. 'We were far too lackadaisical at times', said Lampard.

Chelsea (4-4-2): Cudicini, Paulo Ferreira, Gallas, Terry, Del Horno (Robben), Essien, Lampard, Makélélé, Geremi (Duff), Crespo (J. Cole), Drogba.
Liverpool (4-4-2): Reina, Finnan, Carragher, Hyypia, Riise, Gerrard, Alonso, Sissoko, Kewell (Traore), Luis Garcia (Morientes), Crouch (Cisse).
Attendance: 64,575

There was a lot of gentle sparring between the two sides during the early stages of the game before Chelsea, playing in their sixteenth FA Cup semi-final, seized the early initiative, and if the truth be known, should have taken the lead.

Drogba, in space, was presented with a free header on the eighth minute when Hernan Crespo flicked on Frank Lampard's corner, but the Blues striker put his effort disappointingly wide. Soon afterwards, Drogba was again the culprit for the Premiership leaders when, despite looking suspiciously offside, was presented one-on-one with Liverpool 'keeper José Reina, only to shoot wide after chesting down Lampard's lofted ball.

Chelsea were made to pay for their profligacy almost immediately when, on twenty-three minutes, Liverpool won a dubious free-kick, awarded for a high-footed challenge on Luis Garcia by John Terry as both players went for a bouncing ball.

Rafael Benitez's team made the most of this good fortune as Riise curled his 20-yard free-kick, through the Chelsea wall, and past 'keeper Carlo Cudicini.

Chelsea, who were struggling to break down a well organised defence, were also vulnerable to the counter-attack, and twice Liverpool came close to extending their lead. Terry sold Cudicini short with a defensive header, which saw the goalkeeper and Liverpool striker, Crouch, both injured as they went for the loose ball. They were able to continue after treatment.

On the stroke of half-time, with Liverpool in the ascendancy, Steven Gerrard got free and pulled the ball back from the byline for Garcia, who should have done better than blaze high over the bar.

José brought on winger, Arjen Robben, after the break, and he made an almost immediate impact when his swinging free-kick was headed in at the far post by Terry.

However, the 'goal' was ruled out by referee Graham Poll, who indicated that the Chelsea defender had held down Riise as he rose towards the ball. Straightaway, things got worse for the Blues when the Reds added a second.

In the fifty-third minute, the energetic Garcia seized on a poor header by William Gallas, and expertly half-volleyed the ball into the net in style from 20 yards, with a shot Cudicini stood very little chance of saving.

The Reds were dominant at this stage of the game, with Chelsea looking rather disjointed, and another Garcia volley forced Cudicini into a scrambling save. With the boss gesticulating from the touchline, Chelsea upped their game and, at last, they started to push Liverpool back with substitutes Joe Cole and Damien Duff, the instigators. With twenty minutes remaining, they pulled a goal back. Riise mistimed his attempted headed clearance, and as 'keeper Reina failed to punch the ball clear, Drogba pounced to nod home from close range. What might have transpired had he had done this earlier?

Blessed with a new lease of life, Chelsea went for broke. Robben shot straight at Reina from 6 yards during an enthralling spell in the game and, with Liverpool pinned back in their own half, an equaliser looked distinctly possible. In fact, the Reds had to endure some scary moments, including a late effort by Cole, which almost found its way through.

However, to Chelsea's annoyance, the Merseysiders' defence held firm and Liverpool duly booked their place in the final against West Ham United on 13 May. The game ended 3-3 after extra time, before the Reds won 3-1 on penalties.

CHELSEA 3 MANCHESTER UNITED 0
29 April 2006

Focused Chelsea wrapped up back-to-back Premiership titles with an impressive victory over eight-time champions, and subsequent runner's-up, Manchester United. José knew this was the 'big one', and he certainly got his players fully prepared for another special occasion at Stamford Bridge.

Many said before kick-off that whoever scored the first goal would win the game – and so it proved. Chelsea were, it seemed, ready for a fight from the word go. United weren't so keen. As the game progressed, Chelsea grew stronger and stronger, and in the end could well have won by a much bigger margin ... 5-0 wouldn't have gone amiss.

Chelsea (4-4-2): Cech, Paulo Ferreira, Carvalho, Terry, Gallas, Makélélé, J Cole (Crespo), Essien, Lampard, Robben (Duff), Drogba (Maniche).
Manchester United (4-3-3): Van der Sar, G. Neville, Ferdinand, Vidic, Silvestre, Ronaldo (van Nistelrooy), O'Shea, Giggs (Richardson), Park, Rooney (Evra), Saha.
Attendance: 42,219

Beaten only three times in the Premiership all season, once by Manchester United at Old Trafford in early November, Chelsea were hell-bent on gaining revenge over their arch-rivals, and they certainly produced a championship-winning performance. Amy Lawrence, reporting for the *Observer*, wrote, 'You wait fifty years for a title and then two come along in as many years ... how do you begin to explain that hoisting the Premiership trophy courtesy of a swaggering 3-0 victory over Manchester United does not happen every year?'

Chelsea made sure they retained their title with authority and style. Skipper John Terry took a hefty knock from the boot of Wayne Rooney early on, but he battled heroically through the pain barrier and ended up hobbling. Nothing was going to stop him from being on the pitch as the final whistle blew on his second title.

In midfield, Claude Makélélé was brilliant, demonstrating why Chelsea are ahead of the game compared to United. The Reds never got to grips in central midfield, where Ryan Giggs and John O'Shea were overwhelmed by the Frenchman who dictated play so intelligently.

Joe Cole was also outstanding. A constant menace to Gary Neville, his vibrant display was crowned with the all-important goal that ensured this would be Chelsea's day.

The celebrations were inclusive enough for a delighted José Mourinho to launch a couple of winner's medals into the crowd, as he said 'thank you' for their support during the astonishing home run that had underpinned this campaign, which saw his team fritter away just two points out of fifty-four.

United were bystanders to a Premiership party for the second time in five seasons. Rooney was United's only threat. Cristiano Ronaldo threatened only spasmodically, and once Chelsea had got an early foothold, United were always chasing the champions.

Chelsea went ahead as early as the fifth minute from a set piece. Frank Lampard's corner was flicked on by Didier Drogba, and with United's defence in disarray, William Gallas was alone, unmarked, to head the ball past Edwin van der Sar. José sat motionless and expressionless, as Stamford Bridge burst to life around him.

United's response was vigorous enough, and they were furious when referee Mike Dean failed to stop play during the attack, adamant that Cristiano Ronaldo had been fouled. An eventful, opening ten minutes became even more heated, when Terry was gashed during a full blooded 50-50 tackle with Rooney. The United striker then clattered into Paulo Ferreira, but escaped a booking.

Chelsea were dominant, but Rooney was always a danger. A virtuoso run by the England striker left Terry, Ricardo Carvalho and Ferreira floundering, but he screwed his shot wide. José had told his players before the match that they can't allow a team to come here and take away the cup. 'It's ours. We deserve it', he said.

The industrious Joe Cole was as psyched up as anybody to fulfill his manager's prophesy. He was everywhere, and came within a whicker of increasing Chelsea's lead with an audacious chip that drifted narrowly wide of the far post. Cometh the hour, cometh the moment, cometh the man ... Chelsea's superstar, Joe Cole.

Petr Cech's enormous throw out was chested by Drogba towards Cole, who tricked his way past Rio Ferdinand and Nemanja Vidic before side-footing the ball into the net. This time, a smiling José did allow himself a moment of celebration by jumping and shaking his fists – 2-0, game won.

It was all too easy now for Chelsea, and in the seventy-third minute, centre-back Ricardo Carvalho turned into Franz Beckenbauer, beginning and ending a sweeping move. The Portuguese defender, aided on the way by Lampard and Cole, moved gracefully forward, before letting fly with a swerving right-foot shot that nestled inside Van der Sar's near post.

The whole stadium erupted to acknowledge the goal as the chants of 'boring, boring Chelsea' rang out from the Matthew Harding stand. This was dramatic stuff, and the Chelsea supporters loved every minute of it.

Eight minutes from time, Rooney went off with a damaged foot. But by that time, even he had given up. Chelsea were champions again – and deservedly so.

José may often bristle at a perceived lack of respect from English football supporters, but in one corner of London (SW6) they know when they are on to a good thing.The home fans cheered their hearts out when their man – the 'Special One' – duly stepped out for the trophy presentation.

Fact: Almost a year earlier in May 2005, United suffered the ignominy of providing the guard of honour for Chelsea to walk out at Old Trafford as champions for the first time in half a century, eighteen points clear of the hosts in José's first season in charge. Fergie's men lost the game 3-1.

CHELSEA 4 WYCOMBE WANDERERS 0
(Chelsea won 5-1 on aggregate)
23 January 2007

Chelsea reached their fifth League Cup final with a comfortable two-legged victory over Football League Two side, Wycombe Wanderers. After a 1-1 draw in the first game, braces by Ukrainian striker, Andriy Shevchenko, and Frank Lampard, earned José's team a meeting with London rivals Arsenal at Cardiff's impressive Millennium Stadium.

On a bitterly cold night, it was a warming experience for Shevchenko who was good value for his first-half double as Chelsea overpowered their opponents.

Starting up front for the first time in four games, alongside Didier Drogba, he played well and could easily have scored twice more. Paulo Ferreira, rather than Michael Essien, made way and there was a fifth different name at right-back this season when Lassana Diarra was handed his first start. And keeping goal at the Bridge for the first time since his head injury was Petr Cech, who was making his 100th appearance at senior level for Chelsea.

Chelsea (4-4-2): Cech, Diarra, Essien, Carvalho, A. Cole (Morais) Makélélé, Mikel, Lampard, Ballack (Wright-Phillips), Shevchenko (Kalou), Drogba.
Wycombe (4-5-1): Batista, Martin, Antwi (Stockley), Williamson, Golbourne; Betsy, Doherty, Oakes (Anya), Bloomfield (Torres); Mooney, Easter.
Attendance: 41,591

Shevchenko had a chance in the very first minute, but he glanced Ashley Cole's precise cross beyond the far post. Five minutes in came the first booking – Wycombe's Antwi yellow-carded by referee Mike Dean for going straight through Drogba with an ugly sliding tackle. Lampard then fired over, before Shevchenko saw his well-connected shot blocked by the outstretched boot of Antwi in the fifteenth minute. Thirty seconds later, Baptista spilled Diarra's low shot, but the 'keeper reacted quickest to hook the ball away from 'Shevco' with his right foot.

Chelsea deservedly took the lead in the twenty-first minute. Wanderers' midfielder Tommy Doherty passed across the pitch, straight to Shevchenko, who raced 40 yards downfield before drilling the ball low, past the stranded Baptista for his first goal in seven weeks.

Four minutes later, Mooney had a half-chance for the visitors, but missed a difficult volley at the far post, although Cech was well positioned and probably would have saved the shot.

Ten minutes from half-time, Chelsea were denied a penalty when referee Dean failed to spot Betsy's raised arm in a defensive wall following Michaels Ballack's free-kick. Did he mean it? Some referees would have given a spot-kick, the majority not.

Chelsea, well on top, doubled their score three minutes before the interval. Drogba collected a misdirected pass by Diarra, and floated the ball into the penalty area where Shevchenko connected first time, looping his shot over the advancing Baptista. An effort from Betsy caused a rare moment of pandemonium in the Chelsea penalty area before the half-time whistle sounded.

Chelsea's first chance of the second-half came in the fifty-third minute, but Lampard prodded wide from 6 yards after Shevchenko had teed up his stand-in captain.

Michael Essien was the first Chelsea player to be yellow-carded, after stamping down on the ball in disgust when his strong challenge was penalised, and almost immediately, Drogba powered his diagonal shot wide before Ashley Cole was booked for dissent on the hour.

With Wycombe pinned back, Lampard fired over and Drogba shot straight at the 'keeper while, at the other end of the field, Chelsea's 'keeper, Cech, did well to keep out Oakes's sixty-sixth-minute free-kick, which swerved late. Ninety seconds later, Lampard put Chelsea three up. The midfielder ran onto Shevchenko's high pass, toe-ended the ball over Batista and rolled it into an empty net. The Ukrainian then went close again, and Mikel missed a gilt-edged opportunity for number four when he failed to finish off a Ballack-Drogba move.

Chelsea rounded things off in the very last minute. Lampard fed Drogba, and the skipper was there to take a return pass to score from point-blank range.

Beating a League Two side at home for a place in a major Cup final wasn't the most difficult task José and his team had ever encountered, but in the end it was job well done. Next on José's hit list – Arsene Wenger's Arsenal in the Welsh capital in five weeks time.

CHELSEA 2 ARSENAL 1
25 February 2007

The 2007 League Cup final, played at Cardiff's Millennium Stadium, was the first all-London clash in the competition's history.

The two sides had previously met at the same venue for the 2002 FA Cup final when the Gunners won 2-0. This time it was Chelsea's turn to celebrate victory. Theo Walcott put Arsenal ahead, before Didier Drogba struck twice for José's team with his twenty-seventh and twenty-eighth goals of the season.

En route to the final, Chelsea had knocked out Blackburn Rovers (2-0 at Ewood Park), Aston Villa (4-0 at home), Newcastle United (1-0 on Tyneside) and Wycombe Wanderers (5-1 on aggregate) while Arsenal's route to Cardiff saw them beat West Bromwich Albion (2-0 at the Hawthorns), both Merseyside clubs, Everton (1-0 at Goodison Park) and Liverpool (6-3 in a terrific encounter at Anfield) and North London rivals Tottenham Hotspur (5-3 on aggregate in the semi-final).

Due to train delays caused by a major signal failure, about 2,000 fans arrived far too late to see the kick-off, and this led to many asking the authorities for the game to be delayed. It wasn't, and afterwards Network Rail apologised for the delay and any convenience caused. Unfortunately, quite a few disgruntled supporters who entered the stadium, much later than planned, missed the opening goal.

This London derby was also the last Football League Cup final to be staged at the Millennium Stadium (before the opening of the new Wembley Arena) and it was also the only League Cup final to be played at the Welsh ground with the roof open.

The match itself was interrupted by incidents of Chelsea fans throwing celery in the direction of the Arsenal players. Apparently, throwing celery onto the pitch is a club tradition among Chelsea fans ... is it? And following incidents on the pitch, especially at the end of the scheduled ninety minutes, when three players were sent off by Yorkshire referee Howard Webb, some media outlets dubbed the match the 'Snarling Cup final'.

Chelsea (4-4-2): Cech, Diarra, Terry (Mikel), Carvalho, Bridge, Makélélé (Robben), Lampard, Ballack, Essien, Shevchenko (Kalou), Drogba.

Arsenal (4-4-2): Almunia, Hoyte, Toure, Senderos, Traore (Eboue), Walcott, Fabregas, Denilson, Diaby (Hleb), Aliadiere (Adebayor), Julio Baptista.
Attendance: 70,073

It was all Arsenal early on, as Chelsea's expensive line-up had few answers to Gunners' dynamic midfield trio of Cesc Fabregas, Abou Diaby and Denilson. After a continued bout of activity in the eleventh minute, Petr Cech had to produce a stunning save after Julio Baptista's low shot had zipped through the legs of John Terry.

Chelsea's defence failed to clear the resulting corner, and as the ball broke free, it was collected by teenager Walcott who exchanged passes with Diaby, glided past a flat-footed Ricardo Carvalho, and keeping his cool, slotted the ball into the net with aplomb. This was the seventeen-year-old's first goal for the Gunners at senior level.

Chelsea responded well and equalised in clinical, but controversial fashion, in the twentieth minute, with their first real worthwhile attack. Arsenal's back four pushed forward expecting an offside decision as Michael Ballack played a teasing ball over the top for Drogba. The big striker ran on unmarked to slip the ball under Manuel Almunia.

It was a split decision, given in favour of the attacking player, but Arsenal manager Arsene Wenger was not too pleased, and spent the remainder of the opening half displaying his anger at the assistant referee's failure to raise his flag. Although pegged back, Arsenal continued to push men forward when possible, hitting Chelsea from all angles, and they almost regained the lead just before the interval. A smart passing movement set Jeremie Aliadiere free, but a brilliant intervention by Portuguese defender Carvalho denied the French striker a shot on goal.

The Gunners continued to dominate proceedings and were certainly looking the more attack-minded side during the early stages of the second half. Diaby had an effort saved by Cech, and Fabregas sent his shot inches wide when well placed. Unfortunately, Chelsea lost skipper John Terry midway through the half when he took a boot in the face from Diaby as he tried to finish off a corner floated over by substitute Arjen Robben.

Terry looked to be knocked unconscious, and an air mask was applied to his face to help with his breathing before he was carried off the field on a stretcher and taken to hospital. John Obi Mikel came on as a substitute as José adjusted his on-pitch line-up.

Terry's departure seemed to fire up his teammates, and they finished the game strongly as Arsenal's young legs began to tire rapidly. Drogba had a powerful shot well saved by the diving Almunia, and Frank Lampard produced a dipping long-range effort that crashed against the bar.

With Arsenal under the cosh, and Chelsea beaming in confidence, the game was there for the taking. In the eighty-fourth minute, Robben's cross picked out Drogba who headed past a stranded Almunia to put his side in front to the delight of the massed ranks of blue-clad supporters behind the goal.

Shevchenko thought he had clinched victory soon afterwards, but his strongly-hit shot thundered back off the bar with the well-beaten Almunia grabbing at thin air. With the board showing seven minutes of added time, Arsenal pushed everyone forward in search of an equaliser, and when Mikel clashed with Kolo Toure, several players from both teams, as well as the respective managers, got involved in an ugly on-field scuffle.

Efficient referee Webb sorted it out by brandishing red cards to 'prize fighters' Mikel and Toure, and also handed one to Arsenal substitute Emmanuel Adebayor, as well as showing yellows to both Fabregas and Lampard. The latter said after the game, 'Six of us could have seen red after that fracas.'

An extra four minutes was then added on following the skirmish, before the final whistle was blown to bring the first major trophy of the season to José Mourinho's side who, at the time, were still in the hunt for three other pieces of silverware.

BLACKBURN ROVERS 1 CHELSEA 2
(after extra time)
15 April 2007

With the season slowly but surely drawing to a close, José Mourinho was still quietly confident that his Chelsea side could win four trophies. The League Cup was already sitting proudly in the Stamford Bridge boardroom cabinet, but he wasn't at all afraid to say 'Let's win the lot ... we still have a great chance of capturing the Premiership title, and if we can overcome Liverpool in the Champions League, we could win that as well, and of course, right now we are still in the FA Cup.' At the time of this semi-final encounter against Blackburn Rovers, Chelsea were lying second behind Manchester United in the Premiership and were scheduled to play Liverpool, over two legs, in the Champions League semi-final.

First up for José and his players was a meeting with mid-table Blackburn, managed by former Chelsea player Mark Hughes. For the winners, it meant a place in the first FA Cup final to be staged at the new Wembley Stadium on 19 May.

Chelsea, roared on by some 22,000 supporters at Old Trafford, showed all the qualities they possess, including the odd dash of luck, to beat Rovers after extra time. But it was close, far too close for comfort in fact, for José's men. With seven minutes remaining, and the scores standing level at 1-1, Rovers' wide midfielder, Morten Gamst Pedersen, saw his free header sail wide, and with barely ninety seconds left, John Terry completely misheaded Pedersen's long throw-in, only to be redeemed by an uncanny save by Petr Cech who somehow managed to claw the ball away to safety.

If either of those efforts had gone in, Chelsea would have lost – there's no doubt about that. As it was, they survived and went on to win the game, courtesy of Michael Ballack's left-footed belter.

Blackburn Rovers (5-3-2): Friedel, Emerton, Mokoena, Nelson, Samba, Warnock, Bentley (Derbyshire), Dunn (Peter), Roberts, McCarthy, Pedersen.
Chelsea (4-4-2): Cech, Essien, Terry, Carvalho, A. Cole, Makélélé (Mikel), Ballack, Lampard, Drogba, Shevchenko (Kalou), J. Cole (Wright-Phillips).
Attendance: 50,559

After a fairly quiet first fifteen minutes, when neither goalkeeper was seriously troubled, Chelsea took the lead. Cech kicked long and high downfield. Didier Drogba chested the ball sidewards to German midfielder Ballack who, in turn, rolled an impeccable pass through to Frank Lampard. The England midfielder's first touch was perfect as he glided past New Zealand defender Ryan Nelsen, before angling a low shot past American 'keeper Brad Friedel.

Chelsea looked good, although they were not playing at top speed, and for the majority of the first half, performed with skill and an abundance of confidence. The only flaw lay in their finishing. Ashley Cole and Drogba set up Joe Cole in the twenty-second minute, but, having juggled the ball from left foot to right, he somehow lofted it over the bar. Rustiness perhaps? Definitely yes, as Cole, due to injury, had not started a game for five months

Drogba also should have done better when facing the Rovers' goal 15 yards out, while Andriy Shevchenko was 1 yard away from getting on the end of Makélélé's through pass. Despite Chelsea looking in control, Blackburn still posed a threat, and hitting back strongly, they pounded José's men for a while with both Jason Roberts and Benni McCarthy going close to equalising.

José started to look irritable and fidgety in his technical area as he waved his arms at his players who, for some unknown reason, seemed to have ceased up. Mark Hughes' team looked the stronger as half-time approached, and there was certainly a lot of talking done in the dressing room.

Chelsea should have doubled their lead in the forty-seventh minute, when Drogba squared the ball to Shevchenko who miskicked so comprehensively that the ball flew sideways when he was expected to bury it in the back of the Rovers' net. This was a bad miss.

Blackburn reacted by unleashing all their verve and determination, and just past the hour mark, unmarked Pedersen headed against the post with Cech beaten. Two minutes later, the Norwegian fired across a free-kick from the right. The ball speared towards Cech's near post where Jason Roberts, darting in front of Terry, slipped a low shot home for the equaliser. This rocked the Blues, who had lost their impetus somewhat and certainly looked uncomfortable.

Rovers, to be fair, had the better of the final twenty-five minutes, but Chelsea's defence, with Drogba back helping out at every opportunity, and goalkeeper Cech playing superbly, held firm, while at the other end of the field, Friedel was rarely troubled. In fact, the pause at the end of normal time came as a relief to Chelsea. After José had ripped into his players, they came out at the start of extra time looking far more determined than they had been during the last quarter of normal time.

Drogba, who had been by far Chelsea's best player, had the first shot on goal at the start of extra time but, as the minutes ticked by, it was now getting mighty tense out on the pitch as defenders cleared their lines with huge kicks, rather than delicate passes.

Four minutes into the second period of extra time, one Chelsea substitute, Salomon Kalou, found another, Shaun Wright-Phillips. The wide man cleverly turned Nelsen on the bye-line and drove the ball into the Rovers' penalty area.

Kalou, who had made ground fast, could not quite reach the cross, but the ball ran on and into the path of Ballack, who taking aim, drilled home a sweet left-footer. Chelsea 2 Blackburn 1 – Wembley here we come.

Key substitutions, made at crucial times by José, certainly helped Chelsea to weather the Rovers' storm. And Ballack, who at times tended to drift out of a game, contributed greatly to this semi-final victory. In fact, the experienced German featured in the last ever game at the old Wembley Stadium, when Germany beat England 1-0, and was looking forward to playing in the first FA Cup final at the new arena. He said, after the semi-final win over Rovers,

> We played well, but it was hard work because we didn't control the game as we would have liked. They created some good chances and were unlucky, and it was a good job that our goalkeeper, Petr Cech, was in such good form. Now I'm ready to visit the new Wembley, and I want to win the Cup with Chelsea.

This was Chelsea's seventeenth FA Cup semi-final appearance, as they qualified for their eighth final in the competition overall. Their opponents at the new Wembley on 19 May would be Manchester United, who defeated Watford 4-1 in the other semi-final.

LIVERPOOL 1 CHELSEA 0
(1-1 on aggregate: Chelsea lost 4-1 on penalties)
1 May 2007

In Group A of the 2006–07 Champions League, Chelsea beat, and also lost to, the German side Werder Bremen, 2-1 and 0-1, defeated Bulgarian outfit, Levski Sofia, twice – 3-1 away and 2-0 at home – and overcame Spanish giants Barcelona 1-0 at Stamford Bridge and forced a 2-2 draw in the Camp Nou. They then knocked out FC Porto 3-2 on aggregate in the first round proper, before eliminating Valencia, also 3-2, over two legs in the quarter-finals. Looking good and strong, José's men were certainly confident of reaching the final of the Champions League for the first time in the club's history, having previously lost in successive semi-finals of 2004 and 2005.

Chelsea's opponents for a place in the final, to be staged in Athens in a fortnight's time, were Liverpool, managed by Rafael Benitez, who were sitting in third place, one rung below José's team in the Premier League. But, three days before the first leg at Stamford Bridge, the Merseysiders had suffered a 2-1 loss at Portsmouth, whereas Chelsea, unbeaten in eleven League games dating back to January, had only lost five competitive matches all season. They were bang on form and firm favourites with the bookies to gain an advantage to take to Anfield.

As it was, they did gain an advantage, albeit a rather slender one, after a registering a 1-0 win at Stamford Bridge thanks to Joe Cole's twenty-ninth minute goal in front of 39,483 spectators, some 2,500 below the ground capacity. Liverpool defended well on the night, and José said after the game, 'They (Liverpool) need to score twice at least, and that will be hard. If we get it right, we shall be in the final, not Liverpool. It will be a big night for everyone at Anfield. I'm looking forward to it.'

Liverpool (4-3-3): Reina, Finnan, Carragher, Agger, Riise, Mascherano (Fowler), Pennant (Alonso), Gerrard, Crouch (Bellamy), Kuyt, Zenden.
Chelsea (4-5-1): Cech, Paulo Ferreira, Essien, Terry, A. Cole, Makélélé (Geremi), Mikel, Lampard, Drogba, Kalou (Wright-Phillips), J. Cole (Robben).
Attendance: 42,554

With Salomon Kalou replacing the injured Andriy Shevchenko, and Michael Essien assuming Ricardo Carvalho's place alongside John Terry at the heart of the defence, Chelsea, with that crucial one-goal lead, took the game to Liverpool from the kick-off. And there is no doubt that Josés team looked up for it, and Reds' 'keeper, Pepe Reina, had to be alert early on as Didier Drogba threatened his goal. Liverpool though, slowly but surely, found their feet, and after Steven Gerrard and Peter Crouch had tested Cech, the Merseysiders scored from the first clear chance of the night.

On twenty-two minutes, Joe Cole fouled Gerrard on the left flank and, with everyone expecting the Liverpool skipper to whip in a cross towards the far post, he slid the ball across the edge of the penalty area to his centre-back Daniel Agger, who slammed it first time into the bottom corner of the net. At this stage in the game, Liverpool were good value for their lead in a game that had plenty of excitement, but lacked real quality.

With the scores level on aggregate, Liverpool tended to take their foot off the gas a little, allowing Chelsea into the game and Reina had to beat away a powerful drive from Drogba following Mikel's through-ball.

Chelsea, competing in their third Champions League semi-final in four years, almost went ahead seconds before the break, when Essien just failed to divert a Drogba header past Reina from Frank Lampard's corner. Liverpool then upped their game and had three excellent chances to double their lead after the break. Firstly, winger Jermaine Pennant wriggled his way free on the right and crossed to Crouch, but his downward far-post header was kicked away by Cech, allowing Terry to complete the clearance.

Five minutes later, Liverpool stormed forward in numbers, and a fantastic cross from left-wing back, John Arne Riise, was met by Kuyt whose header crashed back off the bar. After a rare mistake by Terry, stand-in defender Essien bailed out his skipper by launching himself at Pennant's shot to divert the ball over for a corner.

Chelsea were still in there fighting, and conjured up their best move of the half on sixty-five minutes. Lampard combined with Joe Cole to put in Ashley Cole, but Jamie Carragher got ahead of Drogba to turn the cross over the bar from 3 yards. Drogba almost burst through minutes later, but was thwarted by Reina. At the other end, Bolo Zenden tested Cech with a crisp 20-yard strike.

Despite plenty of enthusiasm, neither side could find the all-important match-winning goal in normal time. Chances were rare throughout the extra thirty minutes as well, with both goalkeepers having a relatively easy ride.

It was Liverpool who came closest to scoring, when substitute Xabi Alonso unleashed a rasping 35-yard drive straight at Cech. The Chelsea stopper was well positioned, yet could only parry the ball into the path of Kuyt, who found the net but was rightly ruled offside.

In the second period of extra time, Drogba almost converted Shaun Wright-Phillips' tempting cross, while Kuyt saw his well hit shot beaten away by Cech in the closing moments.

So it was down to a penalty shoot-out, and this is what happened as Liverpool went first:

- Ex-Chelsea star Bolo Zenden scores, sending Cech the wrong way, Liverpool 1-0.
- Arjen Robben's spot kick saved by Reina, diving to his left, still Liverpool 1-0.
- Xabi Alonso nets hard and low to Cech's right, Liverpool 2-0.
- Frank Lampard scores by smashing his shot down the middle, Liverpool 2-1.
- Steven Gerrard coolly fires into the corner of the net to Cech's left, Liverpool 3-1.
- Gérémi's weak shot is saved by Reina diving to his right, still Liverpool 3-1.
- Dirk Kuyt scores, drilling his shot low to Cech's right, Liverpool 4-1.

It was Liverpool who went forth into the Champions League final; Chelsea were out. 'You win some, you lose some… we lost this one hands down', said a disappointed José. The Merseysiders were subsequently defeated 2-1 by AC Milan in Athens.

CHELSEA 1 MANCHESTER UNITED 0
(after extra time)
19 May 2007

Ahead of José Mourinho's first FA Cup final as the manager of Chelsea – and the club's eighth appearance in the final overall – news broke that up to six players could miss what, to most of them, would be perhaps the greatest occasion of their footballing career.

The six players under eye of the club's physiotherapist were named as Michael Ballack (recovering from ankle surgery), Ricardo Carvalho (damaged medial ligaments in his right knee), Andriy Shevchenko (groin problem), Arjen Robben (knee injury), John Obi Mikel and Ashley Cole, although the latter two were responding to treatment and were both expected to be declared for the big occasion. Also, some reports stated that Robben may be used as a second-half substitute, albeit for a few minutes, if required.

Manager José, on learning about these injury worries, smiled and said: 'I might have to play my reserve goalkeeper Hilario up front.'

Of these half-dozen frustrated players, José admitted he felt really sorry for centre-back Carvalho, saying, 'He has been terrific all season and it is very unfortunate that he has to miss this first final at the new Wembley.'

Before the final, it was announced that the Portuguese defender had signed a five-year contract at Stamford Bridge. Wayne Bridge, Michael Essien, Didier Drogba and Ashley Cole had also agreed to stay on longer at the club, and it was understood that both John Terry and Frank Lampard were ready to sign extensions to their contracts as well. And as one supporter hinted, 'If José signs an extension to his as well, that would be brilliant, or am I asking for too much?

As it transpired, both Cole and Mikel were declared fit for the Manchester United clash, with Mikel starting in midfield while Cole was named as a substitute. This meant in the absence of Carvalho, the versatile Michael Essien would be switched into the back four to partner Terry at the heart of the defence. José had no problems whatsoever with this move, saying: 'He'll play anywhere, he loves his football.'

For United's Ryan Giggs, it was to be his seventh FA Cup final, thus equalling Roy Keane's post-war record. The Welshman had played earlier in the 1994, 1995, 1996, 1999, 2004 and 2005 finals. As for Chelsea, they were also the last club to win the FA Cup at the old Wembley Stadium when they beat Aston Villa in 2000.

The 2007 clash between the Blues and the Reds was the eighth FA Cup final in a row involving a London club: Arsenal four appearances, Chelsea two, and Millwall and West Ham United one each.

Before the kick-off, there was an official opening ceremony of the new stadium with Prince William doing the honours, as well as a fly-past by the famous Red Arrows and a parade on the pitch of former FA Cup winners (players), including the Chelsea duo of Ron Harris (1970 captain) and Marcel Desailly (2000) and the Manchester United octet of Denis Law (1963), Lou Macari (1977), Arthur Albiston (1983), Norman Whiteside (1985), Lee Martin (1990), Mark Hughes (1994), Gary Pallister (1996) and Peter Schmeichel (1999).

Chelsea (4-4-1-1): Cech; Ferreira, Essien, Terry, Bridge, Makélélé, Lampard, Mikel, J. Cole (Robben/A. Cole), Wright-Phillips (Kalou), Drogba.
Manchester United (4-4-2): Van der Sar; Brown, Ferdinand, Vidic, Heinz, Carrick (O'Shea), Scholes, Fletcher (Smith), Giggs (Solskjaer), Ronaldo, Rooney
Attendance: 89,826

Referee Steve Bennett (Kent) was in charge of the first Cup final at the new Wembley Stadium, and the attendance of almost 90,000 was the biggest for an FA Cup final since Wimbledon's unexpected, and certainly surprise, 1-0 victory over Liverpool in 1988, when the turn out was 98,203.

Chelsea, aiming to become only the third team to achieve the domestic cup double (after Arsenal in 1993 and Liverpool in 2001) started well, but it has to be said that the opening twenty minutes were marked by cautious play, and a lack of creativity, from both teams.

At twenty-one minutes, Didier Drogba produced the game's first noticeable attempt on goal, hammering a low shot wide from some 30 yards. Ten minutes later, Chelsea's Frank Lampard forced a smart save from United's Dutch 'keeper Edwin van der Sar.

Wayne Rooney, playing well up-field, was twice caught offside as United pushed forward, and Chelsea squeezed the midfield, but the closest they came in the first half was a speculative long-distance effort from Rooney.

At half-time, Chelsea boss José Mourinho made a like-for-like substitution, bringing on winger Arjen Robben for Joe Cole. But before the spectators had taken their seats, Rooney produced the most exciting action of the game, dribbling around two defenders, only to see his powerful shot saved by Petr Cech. Ten minutes later, the former Everton striker carried the ball a good 60 yards towards the Chelsea penalty area, only to be tackled by the last Chelsea defender, Wayne Bridge.

It was all United at this point. Chelsea were on the back foot, and after Ryan Giggs flashed a volley barely 2 feet over the bar from close range, United's Paul Scholes picked up the game's first booking for a reckless foul on Lampard. From the resulting free-kick, Drogba curled the ball around the United wall and off the outside of the near post. With neither side doing enough to score during the scheduled ninety-plus minutes, an FA Cup final went into extra time for the third consecutive year.

It was United who had the next chance, but Giggs, only 3 yards out, failed to get proper contact on the ball and Cech was down quickly to make the save – or did he? Giggs appealed for a goal, claiming that the ball had crossed the line while in Cech's arms, but the linesman (assistant referee) didn't flag and play resumed. However, television replays appeared to show that the ball did actually cross the line, but only after Giggs's momentum had pushed the Chelsea 'keeper backwards into his own goal. Foul? Possibly, but play continued.

Also, after the game, United manager Sir Alex Ferguson claimed that Giggs had been fouled by Essien just before he took his shot. Sour grapes I wonder?

The deadlock was finally broken in the 116th minute, when Drogba played a neat one-two with Lampard on the edge of the United penalty area after receiving the ball from John Obi Mikel. Although losing his balance, the big striker was still able to prod it past the onrushing Van der Sar and into the net. Chelsea picked up three more bookings in the last few minutes as they tried to halt a late United comeback, but Drogba's goal proved to be the last chance of the game as José's side held on to win the coveted trophy for the fourth time.

Drogba led by example against United, produced another Herculean effort as he capped a season that saw him become the first Chelsea player to net thirty goals for twenty years with his second Cup final winner in four months. He was by far, Chelsea's most potent attacking force and his persistence was rewarded with the winning goal, underlining his reputation as one of the most feared strikers in European, and perhaps even, world football. This was Arjen Robben's farewell appearance for Chelsea and a great occasion to say farewell.

CHELSEA 3 BIRMINGHAM CITY 2
12 August 2007

Birmingham City, promoted to the top flight as Championship runner's-up at the end of the 2006–07 season, had only scored one goal in their five previous Premier League games against Chelsea. Though the Midland club's manager, Steve Bruce, wasn't too happy with having to start a new campaign against one of the favourites for the title (Chelsea), he was philosophical when asked 'how will you play ... what formation will you use?' He replied, 'We will play with a ball, as usual, and field eleven players to start with, then we'll see how things transpire after that.'

On the other hand Chelsea – unbeaten at Stamford Bridge in the League since February 2004, and the top flight draw experts of 2006–07 with eleven (seven at home and four away) – were in sight of setting a new record of sixty-four home games without defeat. They were also desperately keen to start the new League season with a victory, having lost on penalties to Manchester United in the FA Community Shield game at Wembley seven days earlier.

With John Terry sidelined with a broken toe, manager José chose Israeli defender Tal Ben Haim (signed from Bolton Wanderers) to play alongside Ricardo Carvalho. Florent Malouda, a £13.5 million capture from Lyon, was named in midfield and Peruvian international striker Claudio Pizarro, signed on a Bosman transfer from Bayern Munich, was preferred to Didier Drogba in attack. Another new face, ex-Reading star Steve Sidwell, was named on the bench.

Chelsea (4-4-2): Cech; Johnson, Ben Haim, Carvalho, A. Cole, Essien (Mikel), Lampard, Kalou, Malouda (Sidwell), Wright-Phillips, Pizarro (Drogba).
Birmingham City (4-4-2): Doyle; Kelly, Djourou, Ridgewell, Queudrue (Parnaby), Larsson, Muamba, Nafti (De Ridder), McSheffrey (Jerome), Kapo, Forssell.
Attendance: 41,590

This turned out to be a very entertaining match, with Chelsea playing some exciting football on a lush surface. José's team dominated huge phases of the game, despite conceding twice in the opening thirty-six minutes. Chelsea should have taken the lead early on, but debutant Malouda fired over when completely unmarked

14 yards from goal. Not overawed initially, Birmingham's opening goal, in the fifteenth minute, came completely against the run of play, and was scored by former Chelsea striker Mikael Forssell.

With Chelsea's defence looking uncertain, defender Liam Ridgewell flicked on Gary McSheffrey's cross into the Finn's path, and he just managed to guide the ball past Petr Cech as he left his line.

José's team, however, equalised two minutes later when the impressive Shaun Wright-Phillips accepted a return pass from the hard-working Malouda before picking out the unmarked Pizarro who marked his Premiership debut with a goal. Though Blues' 'keeper Colin Doyle got two hands on the ball and should have done better.

Just past the half-hour mark, a deft flick through the tightest of gaps by Kalou, and a superbly timed run from Malouda, culminated in the summer arrival from Lyon slipping the ball past Doyle for Chelsea's second. Soon afterwards, another inviting ball was played through to Frank Lampard. With a third goal looking likely, the midfielder opted for placement over power and centre-back Johan Djourou, on loan from Arsenal, managed to block his shot.

Chelsea were finding good attacking positions with ease, while Birmingham, with three of the back four making their senior debuts, looked increasingly ragged. But Kapo, the fourth Birmingham player making his top-flight debut, conjured up a surprise equaliser in the thirty-sixth minute. Rather ineffectual before then, Kapo picked up the ball on the left-hand flank, cut past Glen Johnson, before whipping a low shot across Cech and into the far corner.

Chelsea continued to dictate the play after the interval, and Essien's thumping strike, from Wright-Phillips' lay-off, put the home team back in the fiftieth minute. Once again, though, goalkeeper Doyle was partially at fault due to his poor positioning.

Chelsea continued to press forward, after regaining the lead. Essien fired over. Lampard mishit his shot far too straight. Drogba, on for Pizarro, failed to connect with a low cross, and Kalou's shot on the turn was well saved by Doyle. Birmingham rallied towards the end and Ridgewell came close from a corner, while at the other end, a low Steve Sidwell effort was only inches wide of the post.

For Chelsea boss José, it was a good game, 'My team played well, but because Birmingham did as well as teams who come up from the Championship have a champion mentality.'

Birmingham certainly gave Chelsea plenty to think about, and Steve Bruce was somewhat disappointed because the goals his defence gave away were a bit soft.He said, 'Not many teams come here [Stamford Bridge] and score two goals. We were brave and that's the way we'll have to play'.

The previous unbeaten home League record of sixty-three matches was held by Liverpool, who went from February 1978 to December 1980 without losing at Anfield.

José Departs

After all the pomp and circumstance, the open-bus parades, numerous ceremonies, the receiving of literally thousands of congratulations and barely six weeks and eight games into the new season (on Thursday 17 September 2007, two days after a shock 1-1 home draw with Norwegian side Rosenborg in front of just 24,973 spectators) José Mourinho stunned the football world by leaving Stamford Bridge by mutual consent, with three years of his extended contract remaining.

The decision came after the club held a crisis meeting to discuss the indifferent start to the new season. José's relationship with the club's owner, Roman Abramovich, must also have had a huge bearing on his decision. The former Israel national team coach and Chelsea's director of football, Avram Grant, took over as manager, while José himself agreed a compensation package.

BBC Radio 5 Live football correspondent, Jonathan Legard, understood that José had texted senior players, including skipper John Terry, to tell them he was leaving the club. Meanwhile, Peter Kenyon, Chelsea's chief executive, Bruce Buck, the club chairman, and Eugene Tenenbaum, Abramovich's right-hand man, were all summoned to an emergency meeting at Stamford Bridge to discuss the emerging crisis. In a statement placed on the club's official website, it confirmed that, 'Chelsea Football Club and José Mourinho have agreed to part company today [Thursday] by mutual consent.'

Many of Chelsea's staff and players had been enjoying a relaxing evening at a Fulham Broadway cinema, and by coincidence, were watching the screening of 'Blue Revolution' – a documentary about the Abramovich years. Some senior players, including Terry and Frank Lampard, were absent, and the remainder, except a reluctant Shaun Wright-Phillips, refused to talk to the media. José also attended that same meeting, but as he left Stamford Bridge, he ignored the waiting media and looked decidedly glum.

The Portuguese 'Special One' had done wonders in his three years with Chelsea. Besides guiding his team to the Premiership title, FA Cup glory and two League Cup final victories, he also took the Blues to the semi-final and final of the Champions League in successive seasons, losing on penalties to Manchester United in the 2008 final. He was also voted Premiership 'Manager of the Year' in 2005 and 2006.

1. Chin up. Mourinho gestures from the sidelines. (*Courtesy of Flickr user Ronnie McDonald*)

2. UEFA Champions League
semi-final first leg, Atletico Madrid *v.*
Chelsea, Vincente Calderon Stadium.
(*Courtesy of Press Association*)

Above: 3. Mourinho watches a dispute with the ref. (*Courtesy of Flickr user Ronnie McDonald*)

Below: 4. Mourinho gestures at the players on the pitch. (*Courtesy of Flickr user Ronnie McDonald*)

Opposite: 5. This is a Saturday, May 22, 2010 file photo of Inter Milan's coach Jose Mourinho as he celebrates with the trophy after the Champions League final soccer match against Bayern Munich at the Santiago Bernabeu stadium in Madrid, Spain. (*AP Photo/ Andres Kudacki*)

6. Jose Mourinho holds the ball after it went out of play during the Champions League group E soccer match between Chelsea and Basel at Stamford Bridge stadium in London, Wednesday 18 September 2013. (*AP Photo/Sang Tan*)

7. Jose Mourin is lifted up by h players followir his teams victor at Athletic Bilb vs Real Madrid held at Estadio San Mames in Bilbao, Spain. (*Courtesy of Pr Association*)

Former Chelsea player, Pat Nevin, said, 'José's a very individual man and he thought he should have been the power at the club'.

It was understood that José has been at loggerheads with Abramovich for quite a while. In fact, the Russian billionaire was annoyed at the reluctance of his manager to play Ukraine international Andriy Shevchenko – a player who cost Abramovich a cool £31 million, while his desire to bring in Grant from Portsmouth, to work with the misfiring striker, only served to heighten the tension. Grant was recruited in the summer as Director of Football, and Mourinho is understood to have simmered thereafter.

It is believed that the Chelsea board – Roman Abramovich and his fellow directors – were frustrated by the early results at the start of the 2007–08 season (only three Premiership wins out of six) and also by the pattern of play. They wanted stylish football. They wanted football that appealed to the world and they weren't getting it. José became totally frustrated by the interference. He could not do the job how he wanted, so he left.

BBC sport editor, Mihir Bose, on hearing of José's departure from Stamford Bridge, said, 'It's clear this relationship has been breaking up for a long time.' Former England manager, Graham Taylor, thought the beginning of the end came when Michael Ballack and Shevchenko were brought in, reportedly against José's wishes. Taylor told Radio 5 Live, 'Once you take away the authority the manager has in signing players, you're on a slippery slope. When Shevchenko and Ballack came in, it disturbed the balance of the whole Chelsea team. They never looked fluid in their overall play.'

It is understood that José was given a £10 million pay-off by Chelsea. He was in charge for 185 competitive games as boss; 124 resulted in victories, 40 in draws and only 21 were lost. And for good measure, Chelsea also had a record 60-match unbeaten run in Premier League matches during his initial three years at Stamford Bridge. These statistics clearly justify why José was given the title as the 'Special One' by the Chelsea supporters.

The 'Special One' Returns to Football ... In Italy

After nine months or so out of the game, José returned to football as head coach/manager of the Italian Serie A club Internazionale ... and he made an immediate impact. He signed a three-year deal with the Italian club after succeeding Roberto Mancini, who was surprisingly sacked after leading Inter to a third consecutive Serie A title in 2007–08.

The forty-five-year-old was formally unveiled as the new boss at a press conference on Tuesday 2 June 2008, and in a statement on Inter's website it stated, 'Internazionale announce the arrival of José Mourinho. The Portuguese coach has signed a three-year contract and will work alongside Rui Farias, Silvino and Andrei Villas Boas. The assistant coach will be Giuseppe Baresi.'

Farias, Silvino and Boas were all part of José's backroom set-up at Chelsea, while Baresi was, at the time, head of the Italian club's academy. A spokesman from the Italian club added, 'Thanking Roberto Mancini and his staff for the success obtained in four seasons as the leader of the team. All of Internazionale has the great pleasure to welcome José Mourinho and his coaches.'

José had been heavily linked with the role at Inter, and it was understood he had been taking Italian lessons ahead of any possible appointment. For sure, Inter recruited José to help improve their success in Europe. Despite their domination on the domestic front, they had struggled somewhat in the Champions League, and were knocked out in 2007–08 by Liverpool at the last sixteen stage. 'Serie A is feeling a little tender right now, and perhaps not enjoying its status like before, so having Mourinho joining is a very positive thing,' said Italian football expert James Richardson.

Everyone knew that José had won the UEFA Cup in 2003, and the Champions League in 2004 with Porto, and had twice guided Chelsea to the Premier League title in 2005 and 2006, while also reaching the semi-finals of the Champions League in 2005 and 2007. It was understood that he had 'plenty of money' to strengthen the side, and was reportedly interested in bringing some of his former Chelsea players, including Frank Lampard and Didier Drogba, to Italy.

Internazionale's President Massimo Moratti said, 'I have read lots of names but I have yet to speak with him (José) about the transfer market. I would like to change very little of this squad which has won so much.' Inter's General Manager Ernesto Paolillo responded by saying that there would be 'few, but good players' arriving this summer.

INTERNAZIONALE 2 AS ROMA 2
(after extra time; Inter won 6-5 on penalties)
24 August 2008

José Mourinho's first match in charge of an Italian team resulted in a debut victory, and with it, a trophy, but he said after this nail-biting encounter, that he has 'yet to impose his style on Inter Milan.'

The Serie A champions' latest head coach sat on the bench watching his new team beat AS Roma 6-5 on penalties to lift the Italian Super Cup at the start of the club's seventy-fifth year in football. However, the Portuguese coach was not at all happy at the way his Inter defenders twice surrendered the lead before clinching the season's curtain raiser in a 12-yard shoot-out with the scores locked at 2-2 at the end of extra time. 'No, this is not yet my Inter. I want my Inter to finish the match at the right time; win 2-0 and not by a narrow margin, certainly not on penalties' José told reporters.

Inter Milan (4-3-3): Cesar, Burdisso (Rivas), Zanetti, Maxwell, Maicon, Cambiasso, Luis Figo (Balotelli), Muntari, Stankovic, Mancini (Jimenez), Ibrahimovic.
AS Roma (4-4-2): Doni, Juan, Riise (Tonetti), Mexes, Cassetti, De Rossi, Perrotta (Totti), Pizarro, Aquilani (Okaka), Baptista, Vucinic.
Attendance: 39,919

It was certainly an evenly-matched contest with both teams choosing to attack rather than defend in depth, and, after 120 minutes or so of competitive action, Inter's confident captain, Javier Zanetti, scored the decisive spot-kick past Alexander Doni. In regulation time, Roma's powerful midfielder, Daniele De Rossi, (69 minutes) and striker Mirko Vucini (90), cancelled out goals by Inter's new signing, Sulley Muntari (17), and talented eighteen-year-old front man, Mario Balotelli, (83). And in fact, during the ninety minutes, both teams hit the woodwork, both goalkeepers produced some excellent saves, while Stankovic and Luis Figo (Inter) and Baptista and Aquilani (Roma) all squandered good chances, while Inter's giant Swede, Zlatan Ibrahimovic, twice headed when he knew he should have hit the target.

José Mourinho shared the credit for his first win with his predecessor Roberto Mancini, who had been sacked three months previous despite having won a third consecutive Serie A title, and in an interview, he said 'the match was a good advert for Italian football. They say that it is not possible to play beautiful football here, but Inter and Roma showed exactly the opposite, four goals, lots of chances and enjoyable moves.'

Soon after this victory, José announced that the Ukrainian international, Andriy Shevchenko, who was with him at Stamford Bridge, would be rejoining AC Milan and not Inter Milan, after a miserable two-year stint at Chelsea when he was so often left on the bench by his Portuguese boss.

AC MILAN 1 INTERNAZIONALE 0
28 September 2008

José Mourinho's first Derby della Madonnina (the Milan Derby) ended in a disappointing 1-0 defeat at the hands of arch-rivals AC Milan. And it could have been far worse, a 3-0, even a 4-0 battering looked on the cards at one point, because Inter – who finished with ten men – simply never got going against a well-balanced team that played with a controlled 4-3-2-1 formation, and looked dangerous everytime they crossed the halfway line.

AC Milan (4-4-2): Abbiati, Zambrotta, Maldini, Kaladze, Jankulovksi, Gattuso (Bonero), Seedorf, Ambrosini, Kaka, Ronaldinho (Shevchenko), Pato (Flamini).
Internazionale (4-4-2): Cesar, Zanetti, Maicon, Bundisso, Materazzi (Cruz), Chivu, Mancini (Adriano), Cambiasso, Vieira (Stankovic), Quaresma, Ibrahimovic.
Attendance: 79,057

The only goal of the game was scored by one of the best players in the pitch, Brazilian international Ronaldinho, who found the net with a superbly directed header in the thirty-second minute under the San Siro (Giuseppe Meazza) floodlights. Everyone was anticipating, certainly expecting, Ronaldinho's first goal for AC Milan, one he had promised to the fans before the match. And he duly delivered in style. Launching Kaká down the right wing, he then darted into the middle and patiently waited for the return cross. The ball was duly delivered by his fellow countryman. It sailed high over the head of Esteban Cambiasso and towards 'Ronnie', who timed his jump to perfection. Finding the net with aplomb, the ball flew into the top left hand corner of Julio Cesar's net. The scorer then followed up with his traditional samba jig, with his contagious smile being captured by every photographer inside the ground. *La curva rossonera. Boa vinda Ronaldinho!*

Prior to this, the hosts had played the better and more creative football, whereas Inter lacked commitment, although Mancini shot wide when well placed. Zlatan Ibrahimovic had an effort saved by the legs of goalkeeper Christian Abbiati, while Ronaldinho saw an effort brilliantly saved by the diving Cesar. Some of their close play was tentative, their passing was sloppy and there seemed something missing from their attack.

The second half was fairly even until referee Enzo Morganti started to get busy with his red card, and, in the end, it was a sad night all round for Inter and their supporters. It's never nice to lose a local derby, whatever country or city you live in.

Having seen two of his colleagues sent off – defenders Nicolas Burdisso and Marco Materazzi; the former banished from the pitch for two yellow cards with fifteen minutes remaining, and the latter from the bench for arguing soon after being substituted – Inter's giant Swedish striker, Ibrahimovic, slammed the match official (and the two assistant referees), saying, 'The referee won the game, not AC Milan.' Meanwhile, Inter's boss, José, admitted, 'We made too many errors on the pitch. I don't want to comment on the referee.'

INTERNAZIONALE 3 AC SIENA 0
17 May 2009

Twenty-four hours before taking on AC Siena inside the Giuseppe Meazza Stadium, Internationzale had been declared the 2008–09 Serie A champions after second-placed, and arch rivals, AC Milan had surprisingly lost in the circumstances to Udinese. This defeat left the Nerazzurri seven points adrift of José's Mourinho's team, with only two games remaining. Inter would eventually finish ten points clear of their neighbours Milan (84-74) who took third place behind runner's-up Juventus.

Climbing to the top of Serie A on 9 November, following a 1-0 win over the aforementioned Udinese, Internazionale remained there until the final ball was kicked. This comfortable 3-0 home victory over Siena, in front of nearly 80,000 ecstatic fans, guaranteed José his second trophy as an Italian football club manager and his first as boss of a Serie A winning team.

Internazionale (4-4-2): Cesar (Orlandoni); Cordoba, Chivu, Zanetti, Samuel, Cambiasso, Muntari, Figo (Santon), Stankovic, Ibrahimovic, Balotelli (Mancini).
AC Siena (4-4-2): Curci, Brandao, Portanova, Ficangna, Del Grosso, Galloppa, Codrea (Coppola), Jajalo, Ghezzal, Kharja (Jarolim), Vergassola.
Attendance: 79,439

After a rather disappointing first half, it must be said, Internazionale were ready to walk off the pitch to face a stern talking to from manager José Mourinho. But with barely seconds remaining, and the referee ready blow his whistle, Argentinian midfielder, Esteban Cambiasso, fired his side into the lead, which they just about deserved. Prior to that, neither side had created all that many chances.

Giant Swedish striker, Zlatan Ibrahimovic, and Portuguese wide-man Luis Figo had gotten close for Inter. Likewise, Abdelkader Mohamed Ghezzal and Simone Vergassola had gotten close for Siena, but neither goalkeeper had been tested. Some spectators in the crowd weren't too happy with what they were watching.

Thankfully, things changed for the better after the interval, and, after Stankovic had gone close, Mario Balotelli scored Inter's second goal on fifty-three minutes. Soon afterwards, he should have bagged another, while, at the other end, a long- range drive from Romanian Paul Codrea was easily dealt with by Gianluca Curci, who also comfortably gathered in high crosses from Sulley Muntari and Ibrahimovic.

With time ticking on, and Inter comfortably in control, Ibrahimovic neatly tucked away a third goal on seventy-six minutes to sew up a 3-0 win, although the scoreline flattered Inter. At the final whistle, fans charged onto the pitch to congratulate José's conquering heroes, and afterwards, when all the dust had settled, the 'Special One' simply said 'Job well done.'

INTERNAZIONALE 2 AC MILAN 0
24 January 2010

This was a big win – a decisive win – for José Mourinho's side, who triumphed over their city rivals, AC Milan, despite playing with a man short for more than an hour and actually ending the game with only nine men.

In a highly charged atmosphere, with both sets of supporters roaring on their team, the football wasn't at all brilliant, but it was surely tense, and at times, all rough and tumble, with tackles flying in from all angles. In the end, a joyous José needed no second invitation to revel in this well-deserved victory, but this triumph over his fiercest rivals, inside a seething stadium, would have felt more special than most.

Inter's victory, over an AC Milan side that included out-of-sorts David Beckham, saw the Nerazurri move nine points clear at the top of Serie A, and they did so in the most dramatic circumstances.

Internazionale (4-4-2): Cesar, Zanetti, Lucio, Maicon, Samuel, Santon, Sneijder, Muntari (Cordoba), Cambiasso, Milito (Balotelli), Pandev (Notto).
AC Milan (4-4-2): Dida, Favelli, Thiago Silva, Antononi (Janulovski), Gattuso (Seedorf), Abate, Pirlo, Beckham, Ambrosini (Huntelaar), Ronaldinho, Borrielo
Attendance: 79,796

Inter, who took the lead through Diego Milito in the tenth minute, had Dutch international midfielder, Wesley Sneijder, sent off (for continuously back-chatting to the referee) halfway through the first half, but still had enough left in their locker to claim a crucial victory.

Goran Pandev, with a magnificent free-kick, added a second for José's team to effectively end the game as a contest, but as tempers flared in a tumultuous atmosphere, there was still time for defender Lucio to be red-carded after handling Klaas-Jan Huntelaar's shot in the area in injury time. It didn't matter really, as Ronaldinho missed from the penalty spot kick, Julio Cesar saving low down.

Following the sending-off of Sneijder, José said,

> the decision showed that the authorities are ganging up on his club. Everything was done to try to stop Inter winning the game, but this group is strong and will win the title. When I went into the changing rooms (at half-time) I asked the referee why he sent off Sneijder, and he told me it was because he had applauded him! He asked me what I would do if a player ironically applauded one of my decisions. "No, I replied, I wouldn't have chased him away, we're football men." Hence I understood that this dismissal did not happen just like that.

Sneijder had made an impact within minutes, striking a curling volley against the post from 25 yards. Beckham was shown the first yellow card of the game for a second foul in the space of three minutes, and this set a standard that referee Gianluca Rocchi was obliged to maintain.

The opening goal was inevitable and came in the tenth minute from Inter's top goalscorer, Milito. Ignazio Abate played a half-hearted header back to his goalkeeper, and Milito pounced to fire past the stranded Brazilian, Dida, in the Milan goal. Lucio was then shown a yellow card for simulation, and after Sneijder had applauded the referee, with a certain amount of chin-wagging thrown in for good measure, he took an early bath in the twenty-sixth minute.

The complexion of the game changed from this point on, and Milan started to pose a threat with Ronaldinho claiming a handball against Maicon Sisenando inside the penalty area, which the referee failed to see.

Soon after the interval, the lively Ronaldinho volleyed inches wide before a Beckham cross from the right was met by Marco Borriello, whose 6-yard header flew over. Milito and Pandevs' quick break ended with the latter striking a post on the hour mark, before Pandev clinched victory in the sixty-fifth minute with a finely-struck free-kick.

It was reported after the game that a spectator, a man in his fifties, had died inside the stadium. He collapsed and was attended to by medical staff, who sadly couldn't save his life.

INTERNAZIONALE 2 CHELSEA 1
24 February 2010

It just had to happen – Internazionale drawn against Chelsea in the European Cup.

And predictably, it was José Mourinho who took centre stage in his first match against the club he had led for two-and-a-half seasons. This was an encounter laden with context.

Chelsea's boss at the time, Carlo Ancelotti, had been in charge of Inter's local rivals, AC Milan, for eight years, from 2001 to 2009, and this was the first time he had brought a side back to Milan since leaving Stamford Bridge. In addition, there was the added spice that both managers had won the Champions League before, José with FC Porto in 2004, and Ancelotti with Milan in 2003 and 2007. Both men desperately wanted to repeat the feat with their current clubs. This was set up to be one hell of a contest; everyone (associated with both clubs) was winding each other up. 'Bring it on' and 'Let's get the show on the road' were just two of many comments made before kick-off.

Internazionale (4-3-3): Cesar, Zanetti, Maicon, Lucio, Samuel, Motta (Balotelli), Sneijder, Cambiasso, Stankovic (Muntari), Eto'o (Pandev), Milito
Chelsea (4-4-2): Cech (Hilario), Ivanovic, Carvalho, Terry, Mikel, Lampard, Ballack, Malouda, Kalou (Sturridge), Drogba, Anelka.
Attendance: 84,638

Some spectators were still entering the stadium as Inter, looking sharp and incisive from the word go, took the lead in the third minute.

Thiago Motta won a 50-50 ball just inside the Chelsea half. He fed Samuel Eto'o, who in turn speared a perfect pass through to Diego Milito who, with space afforded by Wesley Sneijder's presence, stepped inside John Terry and beat Petr Cech at his near post.

Despite falling behind, Chelsea were not overawed, and slowly began to assert themselves in the game, claiming the greater share of possession and attacking with good intent. However, they were restricted to a series of long-range efforts by eight hard-working players that formed the Inter defence and midfield. Didier Drogba came closest for the visitors, with a powerful 25-yard free-kick, which beat Julio Cesar but struck the underside of the crossbar, before being cleared to safety.

Drogba's opposite number, Eto'o, then missed a glorious opportunity to add to his tally of eighteen Champions League goals just after the half-hour mark, badly miscuing his shot from 8 yards following Wesley Sneijder's low cross from the left.

The first half ended in controversy, when a mistake in midfield gave Kalou a clear run on goal, but just before he was about to shoot, he was felled by a last-ditch tackle from Walter Samuel.

Referee Mejuto Gonzalez waved away calls for a penalty, but replays showed that Kalou's heels had certainly been clipped by the defender. Kalou's anger turned to jubilation within five minutes of the restart as he equalised.

Chelsea's right-back, Branislav Ivanovic, carried the ball deep into the Inter half of the field, evading at least three challenges, before feeding Kalou 20 yards out. The former Feyenoord midfielder controlled the ball before competently side-footing it past Cesar and into the corner of the net. The teams were level for just three minutes.

Sneijder's swinging cross from the right was headed away by Ricardo Carvalho, but only to Esteban Cambiasso, whose first time shot was blocked by Ivanovic. However, the Inter player was quickly onto the loose ball, and from 18 yards, drilled it low past Cech.

This was a body-blow to Chelsea, coming so soon after they had deservedly drawn level, and it certainly knocked the stuffing out of José's old club as Inter took control. There were intermittent attacks on the Inter goal, the best chance falling to Frank Lampard after some smart work by Drogba and Nicolas Anelka, but Cesar was equal to it.

In the sixty-first minute, Chelsea's 'keeper, Cech, was carried off with what looked like a damaged knee, but it was later revealed he had suffered a minor calf injury. His replacement, Henrique Hilario, produced two good saves as Inter pressed for a third goal. It didn't arrive, despite several attacks, and at the end of the game, José was asked if a single goal first-leg advantage is good enough to take to Stamford Bridge?

With a little grin on his face, and tongue in cheek, he replied, 'We lead 2-1 and if we score again we will win … it's that simple.'

The return leg at Stamford Bridge, twenty days later, turned out to be another tight contest. Again, it was Inter who came out on top, winning 1-0 with a goal scored eleven minutes from time by Samuel Eto'o.

Chelsea disintegrated after going behind, and Drogba was sent off in the eighty-seventh minute by referee Wolfgang Stark, who ruled that the striker had stamped deliberately on Thiago Motta. At the final whistle, Inter fans waved and sang 'Bye bye Carletto' as the Chelsea boss walked down the tunnel.

José had returned to Stamford Bridge to make one last mark on Chelsea's history as they were eliminated from the Champions League at the last sixteen stage, for the first time since 2006. Under José, Chelsea were often accused of having an overly-cautious approach that came at the expense of entertainment, but Ancelotti afforded his players greater licence to be expansive. Unfortunately, his style didn't work against Inter, at home or away.

INTERNAZIONALE 3 CF BARCELONA 1
20 April 2010

Inter Milan produced a fine first-leg display as they came from behind to beat holders Barcelona and take control of their Champions League semi-final. The Spanish giants, who had knocked Arsenal out of the competition in the previous round, were matched kick-for-kick, tackle-for-tackle, pass-for-pass, by José Mourinho's side, who thoroughly deserved their two-goal advantage.

After such an indifferent start, Inter produced a performance of which Barcelona would be proud; pressing high up the pitch and hitting their opponents on the break with pace and incisiveness, having won the ball back with total commitment.

With Lionel Messi somewhat subdued, Inter cashed in on their supremacy in great style, and victory put José and his Italian champions on the brink of a first appearance in the European Cup/Champions League final since 1972.

> **Internazionale** (4-3-3): Cesar, Zanetti, Lucio, Maicon (Chivu), Samuel, Thiago Silva, Motta, Sneijder, Cambiasso, Eto'o, Milito (Balotelli), Pandev (Stankovic)
> **Barcelona** (4-4-2): Valdes, Dani Alves, Pique, Puyol, Maxwell, Xavi, Keita, Busquets, Ibrahimovic (Abidal), Messi, Pedro
> **Attendance:** 78,776

Diego Milito missed an early chance for Inter after Victor Valdes had saved from Samuel Eto'o. It proved costly, as Barcelona, looking strong, went ahead in the nineteenth minute when Maxwell's left-wing cross found Predo, who neatly slotted the ball home to give them a vital away goal. This was Pedro's twentieth goal of the season.

At this juncture, Inter were seeing less of the ball than their opponents, but they were dogged in defence and looked threatening in the final third of the pitch. After Milito bent another chance wide, José's team deservedly equalised on the half-hour mark.

As Eto'o crossed from the right, three Barcelona defenders got sucked into the middle, including right-back Daniel Alves. This allowed Milito to control the ball and turn and tee up Sneijder, who had the freedom of the park to lash in the equaliser.

Suddenly, Barça were being denied space. They were struggling to find anything like their usual fluency as Inter doubled up on Messi while also denying the, usually influential, Xavi, any time on the ball.

Just after the break, Goran Pandev failed, by inches, to latch on to Milito's ball from the right, but it wasn't long before Inter got themselves ahead. Messi lost possession in midfield, and when the ball came to the impressive Milito, he held up play before setting up the rampaging Maicon on the right side of the penalty area, to blast his side into a 2-1 lead. Barça, tried to respond, but Messi's shot, and a header from Sergio Busquets, were well saved by Julio Cesar in the Inter goal.

On the hour mark, José's men took firm control of the match. Breaking quickly, Eto'o found space on the right to cross high into the danger zone. But Sneijder, well placed, completely misdirected his header and turned around to see the unmarked Milito find the net with his effort from point-blank range.

Having looked comfortable early on, Barcelona were now flustered, and even Xavi was misplacing passes, much to the delight of the Nerazzurri faithful. The visitors laid siege to the Inter goal in the closing stages. Messi's 30-yard free-kick forced Cesar to parry, before Alves was denied what appeared to be a good penalty appeal when he was fouled by Sneijder. And to rub salt into the wounds, the Brazilian found himself cautioned for simulation.

As the clock ticked down, Pedro and defender Gerard Pique were both denied by Inter goalkeeper, Cesar. This was a brilliant and famous win.

One reporter wrote after the game, 'They (Barcelona) can be beaten! A tactically perfect game from Inter. "The Special One" beat 'The Special Team'.'

NB: This result gave Barcelona a mountain to climb in the second leg in Catalonia the following Wednesday, as they aimed to become the first team since AC Milan in 1990 to defend their European title. As it was, the Spanish team won 1-0 with a late goal by former Manchester United defender Gerard Pique, but it was Inter who progressed through to the final with a 3-2 aggregate victory.

SUPERCOPPA ITALIANA
INTERNZIONALE 1 AS ROMA 0
5 May 2010

Always eager to win a trophy – no matter for what reason – José was all up for this one. He was, of course, chasing three prizes in only his second season in Italian football, and he wanted this one as much as any of the others ... just to set him up as being top man in Italy. In fact, Inter had won the Supercoppa Italiana in 2005 and 2006, while Roma had lifted the trophy in 2007 and 2008. This was going to be one tight match, an even contest with nothing between the teams – and so it proved.

Internazionale (4-4-2): Cesar; Maicon, Cordoba (Samuel), Materazzi, Chivu, Zanetti, Cambiasso, Thiago Motta, Sneijder (Balotelli), Milito, Eto'o.
AS Roma (4-4-2): Sergio; Burdisso (Marco Motta), Mexes, Juan Silveiro dos Santos, Riise, De Rossi, Pizarro (Totti), Perrotta; Taddei, Toni, Vucinic.
Attendance: 54,929

José Mourinho had a huge smile on his face as he took his seat in the dugout inside the Stadio Olimpico, Rome, prior to kick-off. He had an even bigger one at the final whistle as his Internazionale team beat Roma by a goal to nil in a tension-filled Coppa Italiana final to lift the coveted trophy for the sixth time in the club's history.

Diego Milito scored the solitary and all-important goal, five minutes before the break, as the Nerazzurri claimed their first silverware of the season with the Scudetto and Champions League still up for grabs.

Surprisingly, Roma boss Claudio Ranieri left his talismanic captain, Totti, on the bench while José Mourinho made three changes to the team that had beaten Lazio the previous weekend, bringing in Ivan Cordoba and Marco Materazzi for the Brazilian Lucio, and the Argentine Walter Samuel in defence. The team started with Milito up front, thus relegating Stankovic to the substitute's bench.

Any doubts over the fitness of Dutch midfielder Wesley Sneijder were confirmed when the Dutch playmaker, despite lining up at the tip of a diamond around the centre circle, went off after just six minutes – one of three Inter players who were well and truly clattered, as ex-Inter defender Nicolas Burdisso and Phillipe Mexes decided early on to set the tone for a nervous match with some reckless challenges.

Inter certainly had the best of the first-half chances and went close to an opener when Esteban Cambiasso's measured pass found future Chelsea player, Samuel Eto'o, on the left. The Cameroon forward ghosted past the onrushing right-back Maicon, only to see his angled shot well blocked by the diving Julio Sergio.

Roma came close to scoring from a counter-attack but Inter's 'keeper, Julio Cesar, made a brilliant interception, diving to tip the ball away from the foot of Luca Toni who would have had a simple tap-in from Rodrigo Taddei's low cross.

An annoyed Milito then had a goal disallowed for offside after he had run through to meet Eto'o's forward pass, but there was no disputing his match-winner in the fortieth minute.

Thiago Motta found space and freed Milito with a deft pass. Controlling the ball, the Argentine striker brushed aside a defender, ran into the penalty area, before crashing a fierce right-foot shot high into the top left-hand corner of Sergio's net. Inter survived a scare shortly after the restart when goalkeeper Cesar spilled substitute Totti's free-kick, only for Juan Silveiro dos Santos to head over with the goal wide open in front of him.

At the other end, some bravery by Sergio kept out Mario Balotelli's snapshot and Juan made a last-gasp interception to deny Eto'o. Roma continued to produce chances in an effort to force a draw and take the game to extra time. But when they threatened again, Cesar made a spectacular punch-block from John Arne Riise's bullet of a shot, and Mirko Vucinic drove an angled shot wide when clean through on goal.

The Giallorossi (Roma) ended the game with ten men when Totti was shown a red card by efficient referee Nicola Rizzoli for an ugly challenge on Balotelli, who almost snapped, but was restrained by his teammates.

AC SIENA 0 INTERNAZIONALE 1
15 May 2010

The situation was simple. Going into this last Serie A game of the season, Inter Milan – José's 'Invincibles' to some ardent supporters – stood two points ahead of AS Roma, who had a superior head-to-head record. Therefore victory at Siena would guarantee José's team the title, but a draw or defeat in Tuscany, coupled with a Roma victory against Chievo in Verona, would see the Scudetto go to the Giallorossi. Could this happen?

As it was, nothing less than victory would do for Roma, whose only hope of becoming champions was if Siena – second bottom of the table and already relegated – did them a huge favour and get something off Inter.

In the end it was Inter who triumphed, but only just. They did enough to beat Siena, with a resilient defensive display, to become Serie A champions for a fifth successive season, having won the Italian title in 2006, 2007, 2008 and 2009.

To the relief of 8,000 travelling supporters, hot-shot striker, Diego Milito, scored the only goal of the game in the second half of a tough match played at Stadio Artemio Franchi.

As it happened, Roma also won their final game, 2-0, while Sampdoria claimed third spot in the table, and with it, a place in the Champions League for 2010–11.

This narrowest of wins secured a second Italian League title for José Mourinho, whose Inter side also became the first to win five back-to-back Scudetto since Juventus achieved the feat in the 1930s.

Inter's success also sealed a season's double, following their victory in the final of the Coppa Italia earlier in the month. Next on the agenda, for the treble to be completed, was a match against the powerful German side, Bayern Munich, in the Champions League final.

Siena (4-4-2): Circi, Rosi, Terzi, Cribari (Brandao), Del Grossa, Codrea (Ferreira), Jajalo, Ghezzal, Vergassola, Ekdal, Maccarone (Calaio).
Internazionale (4-4-2): Cesar, Maicon, Materazzi, Samuel, Zanetti, Motta (Pandev), Cambiasso, Balotelli (Stankovic), Sneijder (Chivu), Eto'o, Milito.
Attendance: 15,553

Inside a packed stadium, José's side survived an early scare when Albin Ekdal fired just wide for demoted Siena, who, with the pressure off, were always likely to make it an uncomfortable afternoon for Inter. However, Inter gradually found their feet and were unlucky not to be in front at the interval. Only two excellent saves by Siena's impressive goalkeeper, Claudio Terzi, prevented Milito and Samuel Eto'o from finding the net, while at the other end of the field, Mario Balotelli saw a clever bicycle-kick bounce back off the crossbar.

There was hardly anything to write about for long periods of the first half. Chances were at a premium as defence dominated. To the relief of everyone associated with the club, Inter finally made the breakthrough in the twelfth minute of the second half.

The inventive Javier Zanetti spotted the smallest of gaps in the Siena back four, and cleverly flicked the ball through for Milito who, controlling it perfectly, fired home hard and low with great confidence and technique.

Siena, playing for pride, tried in vain to force an equalizer. This left them short at the back and even in midfield, but although Inter created a handful of chances, they all went begging, with at least four of them seemingly clean cut – much to the annoyance of José. The usually assured Milito fluffed a couple, while Eto'o also missed the target when it looked easier to score.

When the final whistle sounded, it was joy all round. Back in Milan, the celebrations started in earnest and went on for forty-eight hours – even longer in some places. It was wonderful stuff and a delighted Jose lapped it all up.

AS Roma were comfortable winners at Chievo, but victory counted for nothing. Mirko Vucinic put them ahead in the thirty-ninth minute after Francesco Totti had earlier hit a post. Daniele de Rossi doubled their lead on the stroke of half-time, and the Giallorossi held on without any major scares.

Sampdoria won a place in the Champions League with a victory over Napoli, which preserved their unbeaten home record. A goal from Giampaolo Pazzini, early in the second half, sealed the points as they saw off the challenge of Palermo to join Inter, AS Roma and AC Milan in Europe's elite club competition for 2010–11.

INTERNAZIONALE 2 BAYERN MUNICH 0
22 May 2010

Two goals by hot-shot striker Diego Milito made José 'Mighty in Madrid', as his impressive Internazionale team brushed aside the Germans with a wonderful display of power and skill in the Bernabéu Stadium in Spain's capital city. This was Inter's first Champions League victory, and their first major European title success for sixteen years since winning the UEFA Cup in 1993–94. They had previously won the former European Cup in successive seasons of 1963–64 and 1964–65.

Of course, this win also brought Inter the treble, which was a great achievement for the manager himself and his players, the coaches and indeed, everyone associated with the famous Italian club. 'Un risultato riconsegnati brillante e meraviglioso. Grande gioia.'

En route to the final, Inter had played Barcelona on four occasions – twice at the group stage, drawing 0-0 and losing 2-0, and twice in the semi-final, winning 3-1 at home and losing 1-0 away. In between times, they beat Chelsea at home and away (3-1 on aggregate) and likewise CSKA Moscow (2-0 on aggregate).

Bayern Munich (4-4-2): Butt, Lahm, Van Buyten, Demichilis, Badstuber, Hamit, Alintop (Klose), Van Bommell, Muller, Schweinsteiger, Robben, Olic (Gomez).
Internazionale (4-3-3): Cesar, Maicon, Zanetti, Lucio, Samuel, Chivu (Stankovic), Sneijder, Cambiasso, Eto'o, Milito (Materazzi), Pandev (Muntari).
Attendance: 73,170

Full strength Inter – without a single Italian in their starting line-up – started the game somewhat cautiously. However, one could sense that, given the chance, the opportunity, a sniff of a goal, they would break with power and conviction and would quickly get three or four men forward, even five if need be.

Bayern, featuring five home-born players, all of them full internationals except French star Franck Ribery, looked anxious. It was plain to see that every time there was a chance, a pass was swung out to Arjen Robben on the right wing. But José had planned to counter this ploy, and as soon as the Dutchman got hold of the ball, two Inter players were on him in a flash, sticking to him like leeches. The wide man struggled to get his left foot going and, as a result, Bayern had to change their plan of attack. After half-an-hour or so of pensive play from both teams, with very few chances being created, it was the traditional route-one routine that brought Inter their first goal.

In the thirty-fifth minute, 'keeper Julio Cesar's extra-long downfield clearance, straight from his right hand, was cleverly headed on by Diego Milito to holding midfielder Wesley Sneijder, who immediately returned the ball into the striker's path. In a blink of an eye, the in-form Argentine hitman let fly with a right-foot bullet, which soared past Hans-Jorg Butt into the Bayern net. A wonderful goal. Inter were on their way to glory. After this, the Germans pushed more players forward, mainly using both flanks, but rarely going directly through the middle, and this played right into Inter's hands.

José's men remained in full control, although Bayern did have a couple of half-decent chances, so too did Inter referee Howard Webb, turning down a penalty claim by Eto'o. And it was José's men who delivered the killer blow, claiming a second goal in the seventy-first minute.

'Man of the Match' Milito, anticipating what would happen, was quickly on the move between defenders. He collected Samuel Eto'o's pass in his stride, side-stepped his closest marker, Daniel van Buyten, before cracking an unstoppable shot past Butt. This was another super strike by a super player. That was it. Bayern couldn't do anything more. Inter sat back, held the fort and ran out comfortable winners. A delighted José had triumphed again, and what a way to say farewell and thank you to everyone associated with Internazionale, by winning the greatest club prize available.

Hard-tackling Bayern captain, Mark van Bommell, conceded Inter was the 'most effective team', referring to the success of Inter's counter-attacking tactics. Everyone associated with Internazionale did not know, at this stage, that their influential leader, José Mourinho, would shortly be leaving Italian football for Spain's La Liga, to take over at the Estadio Santiago Bernabéu, home of Real Madrid, the scene of his latest achievement. But within forty-eight hours, it was officially announced that this would be the case – so it was *'addio speciale - e ringrazio.'* There would be a few more prizes to come in future years for the manager who, at this time, everyone around Europe and even the world, was calling the 'Special One'.

REAL SOCIEDAD 1 REAL MADRID 2
18 September 2010

Having met his 'new' Real Madrid players – and a few hundred supporters as well – José Mourinho arranged eight pre-season friendly matches at home and abroad to get acquainted with the team, the coaching staff and everyone connected to the playing side of the club.

Starting off with a short trip to the USA, Real took on, and beat, both Team America and LA Galaxy by the same score of 3-2. His third match in charge saw Real defeat Bayern Munich 4-2 on penalties to win the Beckenbauer Cup in Germany; the fourth friendly resulted in a 1-1 draw with Standard Liege in Belgium. This was followed by a 3-1 victory over Heracles in the annual Cuidad de Alicante Trofeo competition in Spain. The Argentinian club, Penarol, were beaten 2-0 at home for the Bernabeu Trophy in game number six. A practice match against the club's 'C' team came next, and ended in a 2-1 win before the eighth and last warm-up game finished level at 2-2 away to Murcia.

There were no serious injuries whatsoever in the pre-season build-up, and José was able to field his strongest team for the opening La Liga fixture against Mallorca in Palma. Unfortunately, the players didn't perform as expected and the game ended in a 0-0 draw. José was not totally disappointed, saying: 'Our opponents defended very well. We simply didn't get out of the blocks. You will see better performances in future.'

And so it proved, as Real went out and won their first La Liga game under José in front of 30,000 fans twenty days later, beating a resolute Real Sociedad side 2-1.

Real Sociedad (4-3-3): Bravo, Gonzalez, Ansotegui, De la Bella, Martinez, Aranburu (Sutil), Gurierrez, Griezmann, Prieto, Tamundo (Agirretxe), Zurutuza (Viguera).
Real Madrid (4-4-2): Casillas, Ramos, Carvalho, Pepe, Marcelo, Alonso, Khedira, Di Maria (Granero), Ronaldo, Higuain (Benzema), Ozil (Diarra).
Attendance: 30,202

There was plenty of action at both ends of the field during an entertaining first half, but unfortunately no goals to report. Madrid had most of the play, Angel Di Maria having a shot saved low down by Claudio Bravo, Cristiano Ronaldo drove a free-kick a yard wide, and Xabi Alonso had his right-foot squirter saved by the Sociedad 'keeper. The hosts, always a threat on the break, responded well, and a header from Antoine Griezmann flew a foot over Iker Casillas's crossbar, while Xabier Prieto fired across the face of the Madrid goal.

After Ronaldo had gone close, soon after the restart, Madrid took the lead on fifty-one minutes. Mesut Ozil fed a short pass to Di Maria on the left. He cut inside and scored with a stunning right-footed shot, the ball flying high past helpless 'keeper, Bravo, into the roof of the net. This was a truly wonderful goal.

Two minutes later, Alonso's 25-yard effort flew high and wide, and not too handsomely, into the spectators behind the goal. After Ronaldo had two free-kicks both charged down in quick succession, Sociedad equalised on sixty-two minutes.

Raul Tamudo, darting through a static Madrid back-line, totally unmarked, diverted Griezmann's fast, low free-kick into the net from 3 yards. Five minutes later, the impressive Griezmann shot inches wide, but Madrid weathered the storm and in the seventy-fourth minute, after five free-kicks had been awarded in quick succession by fussy referee, Antonio Miguel Lahoz, (he blew up for twenty-eight during the course of the game) Ronaldo's 20-yard dead-ball drive struck defender Pepe and flew into the top right-hand corner of Bravo's net to put José's side back in front.

The home side pressed for an equaliser, but Madrid's defence held firm, and late on substitute, Karim Benzema, went close to increasing his side's lead with two good efforts. José and his team were on the march.

CF BARCELONA 5 REAL MADRID 0
20 October 2011

José Mourinho always said that his side would lose one day, but he certainly never expected to suffer such a heavy and humiliating defeat like the one his Real Madrid side suffered at the hands of their arch-rivals Barcelona at the Camp Nou.

After enjoying the greatest start of any coach in Real's illustrious history, José saw his team battered and bruised, and in the end, completely out-witted, out-fought and out-played by Barça who, at times, produced some quite brilliant attacking football with the likes of Lionel Messi, Iniesta, and Xavi displaying skills some spectators had never seen before and perhaps will ever see again.

Barcelona (4-4-2): Valdes, Dani Alves, Puyol, Pique, Abidal, Iniesta, Xavi (Keita), Busquets, Messi, Villa (Bojan), Pedro (Jeffren).
Real Madrid (4-4-2): Casillas, Ramos, Carvalho, Pepe, Marcelo (Arbeloa), Alonso, Ozil (Diarra), Khedira, Di Maria, Ronaldo, Benzema.
Attendance: 98,255

This emphatic 5-0 victory for the Catalan club was described by José as 'a historically bad result' for his club. Indeed it was, at that time, the worst defeat he had suffered in his managerial/coaching career.

Cheers and olés rang round the stadium when the final whistle was sounded. Minutes before, it had been boos all round for Real's Sergio Ramos who, not for the first time in his career, was sent off for a wild scythe at Leo Messi, which led to an irate José moving from his seat on the bench, pointing and accusing the Argentine forward of play-acting again. But the result was plain to see, and there is no doubt whatsoever that the Barcelona team that gave Real a right old roasting was genuinely something special. Pep Guardiola's side was, in truth, imperious. The ball control of every outfield player, even the four defenders, was breathtaking at times. The movement of the midfield quartet and main strikers was absolutely superb. Real simply couldn't cope. They were second best.

The game proved to everyone, quite clearly, that the man himself, Lionel Messi, was by far the best player in the world, despite his diving antics. Although he failed to find the net – for the first time in ten matches incidentally – his overall performance, like those of his colleagues, Andrés Iniesta, Xavi Hernández and Sergio Busquets, was sublime. Admittedly, he went on far less dribbling forays than normal. There were fewer tricks and fantasies. Instead there was a stunning assuredness and impeccable precision in his passing. He certainly controlled the game for a long period, having a hand in four of the goals as he was asked to drop back from his usual forward role into centre-field by Guardiola.

In contrast, Real's top man, Cristiano Ronaldo, had never scored against Barcelona up to this time. He threatened early on, but generally struggled, simply because no one could get hold of the ball and get it to him.

Xavi, the ideologue behind Spain's World Cup success in 2010, opened the scoring after just nine-and-a-half minutes. Messi, receiving a short pass from Xavi, switched the ball out to Iniesta and his precise pass into the box found Xavi, although it fortuitously bounced off his heel before managing to twist and fire a volley past Iker Casillas.

Barcelona, despite playing some rather risky passes in tight corners, soon got the Camp Nou crowd roaring olés as they swept the ball about, using 5-yard, 10-yard, sometimes 20-yard passes to cut through Real's midfield and defence.

It was no surprise when Real fell two behind in the eighteenth minute. Xavi speared a wonderful diagonal ball out to the left. David Villa collected it and delivered a high cross that Casillas could hardly reach. As the ball squirmed free, Pedro got ahead of Marcelo to push it over the line. Almost immediately, it should have been 3-0 when Iniesta's sumptuous assist found Villa clean through, but he was fractionally offside.

Real saw very little of the ball during the first half, but when they did have possession they broke quickly, with Ronaldo flashing one effort just wide and whipping a free-kick past the post. Before the interval, he appealed for a penalty, only the referee, Iturralde González, felt the Portuguese forward had looked for the penalty. Replays suggested otherwise. But in the end it was academic and there could be no complaints.

Between them, Messi, Pedro and Villa made a pig's ear of a superb opportunity at the start of the second-half, and after Messi had a goal disallowed for offside. Xavi, after side-stepping Casillas, could only hit the side netting. Barça came again, and in the fifty-fifth minute, Messi played in Villa who, sneaking behind Pelé, made no mistake with an excellent finish, thus claiming his seventh goal of the season. Seconds later it was 4-0, as the brilliant Messi, once more, slipped the ball though to Villa, who just managed to toe-poke the ball home from close range.

There was still more than thirty minutes remaining. For Madrid and José, it was an eternity. Barcelona barely let them see the ball, never mind touch it. Barcelona added a fifth, three minutes into stoppage time, when Jeffrén Suárez, who had been on the pitch for barely three minutes, finished off Bojan Krkic's cross to complete a miserable night for José's team.

On the night, Barcelona completed 636 passes to Real's 279. 'They could have played with two balls', wrote reporter Roberto Palomar. In fact, during the second half, Madrid barely mustered a meaningful attack. 'We were rubbish, absolute rubbish' said manager José, who added, 'I don't want to see anything like this again.'

NB: This was the fifth time Barcelona had defeated Real Madrid 5-0. Beyond 1934–35 and 1944–45, two times linger in the memory. The 1973 team, led by Johan Cruyff, the player, and the 1994–95 'Dream Team' orchestrated by Cruyff, the head coach. No one could watch this battering of 2010 and not recall Cruyff or indeed, Romário!

REAL MADRID 5 REAL SOCIEDAD 1
24 March 2012

In this game, Portuguese superstar, Cristiano Ronaldo, set a new Real Madrid scoring record for reaching the milestone of 100 goals in Spanish La Liga history in the quickest time by netting twice as his club rebounded from consecutive draws to thrash Real Sociedad 5-1 in the Estadio Santiago Bernabéu.

Prior to this game, Real had been struggling up front. However, after José had given his team a stern talking to – a roasting in layman's terms – everything ran smoothly against what proved, at the time, to be difficult opponents who always looked likely to score. Yet, having said that, if certain other Real players – Argentine striker Gonzalo Higuain and Frenchman Karim Benzema especially – had put their shooting boots on, the final score could well have been in double figures.

Real Madrid (4-3-3): Casillas, Ramos, Varane, Marcelo, Arbeloa, Alonso, Khedira (Sahin), Ronaldo (Jese), Benzema (Coenträo), Higuain, Kaka.
Real Sociedad (4-5-1): Bravo, Demitov, Martinez, Gonzalez (Zurutuza), De la Bella, Cadamuro (Pardo), Aranburu, Illarramendi, Prieto, Griezmann, Agirretxe (Vela).
Attendance: 79,892

An early attack by the visitors saw Íñigo Martinez go close, with a right-footed effort from just inside the box. Real snapped into overdrive almost immediately. After some smart approach work by Benzema, his co-striker, Higuain, pounced to fire Madrid into a sixth-minute lead.

Home centre-back, Raphael Varane, joining his front men, headed over as Madrid pushed forward on the counter-attack. Sociedad looked dangerous, and Imanol Agirretxe, given space, forced Iker Casillas into a diving save. Then, in the space of three minutes either side the half-hour mark, Cristiano Ronaldo was unlucky for Madrid, first with a splendid drive, which was well saved by Bravo, following up with a decent header from a deep cross by Sergio Ramos, which flew inches wide.

In the thirty-second minute, Madrid scored a second goal. The Brazilian Kaka cleverly found Ronaldo, who controlled the ball brilliantly before netting with a low right-footer past Bravo. This was his 100th goal for Real at competitive level, and it came in record time, in the fewest number of matches

Ferenc Puskas formerly held the record for the fastest 100 goals for Real, topping the century mark in his 105th appearance for the club in the 1960s. Ronaldo needed just ninety-two games to score his first hundred.

Almost immediately, Sociedad's Antoine Griezmann headed narrowly wide before the huge crowd saw two goals scored in the space of just fifty-five seconds. In the fortieth minute, Xabi Alonso's sweeping crossfield pass from the right was met, and subsequently put away, with sweet aplomb by Benzema, but straight from the restart, and totally out of the blue, Xabi Prieto latched onto De la Bella's measured pass to reduce the deficit by one.

Early in the second-half centre-back Varane, who once more ventured up field, headed Alonso's cross wide (he should have scored) before Real went 4-1 up in the forty-ninth minute. German midfielder Sami Khedira's angled through ball found Benzema, who took aim and scored with a right-footed shot from 15 yards. Sociedad tried again. De la Bella fired wide and Griezmann had an effort saved by the impressive Casillas, before Ronaldo, with his deadly right foot, scored a fifth goal – and his 101st – for Madrid after Higuain had created the opening.

During the last half hour or so, Griezmann (twice, once with a powerful header) and Aranburu went closest for Sociedad, while nineteen-year-old Jesé Ruiz, workhorse Benzema (before being substituted in favour of Fabio Coenträo), Higuain, Coenträo himself, and the overlapping Marcelo, with the last worthy effort of the game, all tested Bravo to the full.

This was a very solid performance by Real Madrid who had 61 per cent of the play, a total of nineteen shots and headers on goal. This time José was rather more pleased with what he had seen out on the pitch.

BAYERN MUNICH 2 CHELSEA 2
(after extra time - Bayern won 5-4 on penalties)
30 August 2013

The first nine penalties in the shoot-out, at the end of 120 minutes in Prague, were all scored before Chelsea's recalled striker Romelu Lukaku's effort was saved, by Bayern goalkeeper Neur, to deny José Mourinho yet another trophy on his return to the club after a six-year absence.

Fernando Torres gave the Blues an early lead. His effort was cancelled out by Franck Ribery's goal at the start of the second half. Though reduced to ten men when Ramires was sent off before extra time, Chelsea looked the better team. They regained the lead through Eden Hazard, only for the Germans to equalise with just forty-five seconds remaining in the match.

Bayern Munich (4-4-2): Neuer; Rafina (Martinez), Boateng, Dante, Alaba, Lahm, Kroos, Robben (Shaqiri), Muller (Gotze), Ribery, Mandzukic.
Chelsea (4-5-1): Cech; Ivanovic, Cahill, Luis, A. Cole, Lampard, Ramires, Schurrle (Mikel), Oscar, Hazard (Terry), Torres (Lukaku).
Attendance: 17,686

The meeting between the 2013 European champions, and the previous holders of the title, added some spice to this early season encounter at the Eden Arena in the picture-postcard city of Prague. Inside the first few minutes, Chelsea's 5,000 supporters saw Bayern striker Mario Mandzukic plant an early far-post header wide and shoot straight at Petr Cech.

The Blues' backline was stretched again soon afterwards, when Bayern switched play quickly, though Ribery made a hash of his delivery into the area.

It was in stark contrast to the move which saw Chelsea take the lead in the seventh minute. Hazard, at his very best, cruised through the centre of the Bavarian midfield and slipped a pass wide to André Schurrle, who pulled the ball back for Torres to volley hard and low past Neuer, from 15 yards. Torres then fired high and wide in Chelsea's next attack, while at the other end, Cech saved twice in quick succession from the dangerous Ribery. Gary Cahill then deflected another Bayern effort wide, but the Chelsea defender was harshly booked for an aerial challenge on Thomas Muller.

Bayern looked strong at the start of the second half, and it came as no surprise when Ribery equalised with a 25-yard drive in the forty-seventh minute. Arjen Robben then fired over, while Oscar let the ball run away from him when well placed, Neuer diving at his feet.

In the seventy-sixth minute, Branislav Ivanovic headed against the Bayern crossbar following David Luiz's flick-on. The Chelsea defender then saw an effort saved by Neuer before Ramires was sent off, dismissed in the eighty-sixth minute, for a block-tackle on Gotze. This was a harsh decision by referee Jonas Eriksson from Sweden.

Nevertheless, Chelsea battled on and were looking well-assured as the game went into extra time. In fact, two minutes into the added half-hour, Hazard netted with a ferocious drive from distance to put his side 2-1 up. Bayern were stunned, but they hit back hard, and Cech saved twice in as many minutes. Lukaku, on for Torres, went close for Chelsea who were hanging on, until forty-five seconds from the end of play, when, following some uneasy defending, Martinez pounced to net a last gasp equaliser for Bayern.

And so to a penalty shoot out. Bayern went first, scoring through Alaba 1-0. After that further spot-kicks were scored, in turn, by Luiz 1-1; Tony Kroos 2-1, Oscar 2-2, Philip Lahm 3-2, Frank Lampard 3-3, Ribery 4-3, Joe Cole 4-4 and Shaqiri 5-4 before Lukaku's miss.

CHELSEA 6 ARSENAL 0
26 March 2014

Chelsea kept their Premiership title hopes alive, while at the same time severely denting Arsenal's chances with this emphatic victory at Stamford Bridge. The prelude to this London derby was celebratory for the Gunners as it was manager Arsène Wenger's 1,000th game in charge. But all the pomp and glitter were shot down early on as Samuel Eto'o and André Schurrle both found the net inside the first seven minutes.

At sixteen minutes, it was 3-0 when Alex Oxlade-Chamberlain handled Eden Hazard's shot inside the penalty area. The Belgian scored from the spot, but only after referee Andre Marriner had mistakenly sent off Arsenal's left-back Kieran Gibbs. The irresistible Oscar added two more goals, one just before half-time and another in the sixty-first minute, before Mohamed Salah burst through a flat back four to make it 6-0 ten minutes later.

Arsenal are well and truly battered on a day when everything went to order for José and Chelsea on the pitch.

Chelsea (4-5-1): Cech, Ivanovic, Terry, Cahill, Azpilicueta, Luiz, Matic, Oscar (Mikel), Schurrle, Hazard, Eto'o (Torres).
Arsenal (4-4-2): Szczesny, Sagna, Mertesacker, Koscielny (Jenkinson), Gibbs, Arteta, Oxlade-Chamberlain (Flamini), Rosicky, Cazorla, Podolski (Vermaelen), Giroud.
Attendance: 41,614

Three chances were created in the opening four minute – two by Arsenal – before Eto'o put Chelsea in front. Schurrle broke clear and fed Eto'o, who cleverly switched the ball onto his left foot, before curling a sweet shot beyond the diving Wojciech Szczesny into the far corner.

Chelsea came again, and 100 seconds later, Nemanja Matic's measured pass found Schurrle on the corner of the area. The German controlled the ball before confidently drilling a low cross-shot past Szczesny. The score was 2-0.

It had been a great start for Chelsea but a poor one for Arsenal … and it got worse.

In the seventeenth minute, a shot from Belgian international, Eden Hazard, was handled by the diving Oxlade-Chamberlain, and referee Marriner pointed to the spot. Then, amid confusion, he sent off the wrong player. As it was, an unruffled Hazard converted the penalty and Arsenal were up against it big time.

To their credit, the Gunners battled well in midfield, matching Chelsea kick-for-kick, tackle-for-tackle, but they were undermanned, and a deflected drive from Brazilian defender, David Luiz, forced a fine reaction save from Szczesny, who then denied Schurrle with another smart stop. Three minutes before half-time, substitute Fernando Torres (who had replaced Eto'o after just ten minutes) got to the byline and squared the ball for the unmarked Oscar to fire high into the net from 6 yards.

Game over. Arsenal were now completely down and almost out. And for the record, this was the first time Chelsea had scored four goals in the first half of a Premiership game since April 2012, when QPR were their opponents.

Marauding Chelsea started the second half just as they had ended the first – on a charge. Torres weaved past two defenders, but saw his shot blocked by Vermaelen, and Szczesny parried Luiz's effort from the rebound. Arsenal had a decent spell of control just before the hour mark, and a shot from Santi Cazorla almost caught Petr Cech unawares.

Playing with ten men against Chelsea is no easy matter, and in the sixty-sixth minute, Oscar's low drive flew past Szczesny and found the far corner of the net: 5-0. Five minutes later, Salah, looking for and finding space, was released through the middle. He kept his cool, took aim and drove his shot past Szczesny to make the score 6-0. The Gunners had been well and truly shot down.

As the crowd chanted 'easy, easy', Chelsea pressed for more, but Arsenal defended resolutely and threatened twice late on through Vermaelen and Tomas Rosicky. This was a terrific win for Chelsea – their biggest over Arsenal in terms of goal difference, and for the record, it was José Mourinho and Chelsea who beat Arsene Wenger in his 500th game in charge of Arsenal, in 2005.

CHELSEA 1 SUNDERLAND 2
21 April 2014

José Mourinho suffered his first home League defeat as Chelsea manager against a team battling to stave off relegation from the Premier League.

The first victors at Stamford Bridge in José's two stints as a head coach/manager were Gus Poyet's Sunderland, who stunned everyone by producing a gutsy, determined and, in the end, thoroughly workmanlike performance.

Prior to the game, the Portuguese boss had enjoyed a seventy-seven-match unbeaten run on home soil. But this defeat came as a shock, not only to José and Chelsea football club, but to everyone associated with the game. It was totally unexpected, but all credit to the Wearsiders who were good value for their win.

Paraguayan Poyet had done his homework, his players responded, and this victory set Sunderland on their way to safety, while at the same time, the defeat seriously dented Chelsea's championship challenge. Chelsea took an early lead through Samuel Eto'o, but Sunderland rallied back with goals from Connor Wickham and a penalty by Fabio Borini.

Chelsea (4-2-3-1): Schwarzer, Ivanovic, Terry, Cahill, Azpilicueta, Matic, Ramires, Salah (Schurrle), Oscar (Demba Ba), Willian, Eto'o (Torres).
Sunderland (4-4-2): Mannone, Vergini, Brown, O'Shea, Alonso, Larsson (Celustka), Cattermole, Colback, Johnson (Giaccherini), Wickham (Altidore), Borini.
Attendance: 41,210

This shock result – and it certainly was a shock against the Premiership's bottom club – left second-placed Chelsea still two points behind leaders Liverpool who, at the time, had a game in hand over José's team against another relegation-threatened side, Norwich City. But more importantly was the fact that Chelsea had to visit Anfield before the end of the season for what everyone was saying would be the Championship decider – a real six-pointer. As we know, things would change dramatically before the last ball was kicked. Meanwhile, Sunderland, who had surprisingly claimed a vital point away at title-chasing Manchester City in midweek, were in reasonably good form when they arrived at Stamford Bridge.

While the result was a huge coup for the Black Cats, it represented a devastating blow for José, who then had to rouse his men for their trip to Madrid for the first leg of their Champions League semi-final against Atlético in four days time.

Without their top marksman, Eden Hazard, who was out injured, the bare fact was simple as, once again, the Chelsea boss was left lamenting the inadequacies of his other strikers with only one goal being scored from thirty-one chances.

Chelsea began the match confidently, and Samuel Eto'o capitalised on some slack Sunderland marking from a corner to open the scoring after just twelve minutes.

Willian's well-delivered left-wing corner, fired into the heart of the penalty area, was met by the Cameroon forward, who had darted in front of Lee Cattermole to claim his twelfth goal of the season from close range.

Sunderland's equaliser also came from a flag-kick. The ball was played directly to left-back Alonso, who, with acres of space on the edge of the area, sent in a low drive, which was parried by Aussie goalkeeper, Mark Schwarzer. It was Connor Wickham who reacted quicker to beat John Terry to the ball and net his third goal in a week.

Chelsea, having the better of the exchanges, were denied a goal on the half-hour mark when Nemanja Matic was judged to have fouled Jack Colback as he rose to head the ball down for Terry to sweep home on the volley. Shortly afterwards, Sunderland were saved by the woodwork as 'keeper Vito Mannone somehow managed to deflect Branislav Ivanovic's header from point-blank range onto the underside of the bar.

With the visitors coming under severe pressure, Mannone kept them in the game, producing fine saves to deny Matic, Mohamed Salah and Willian in the space of ten minutes. In a frantic end to the half, two penalty appeals were turned down by referee Mike Dean as Alonso appeared to handle inside the box, and Sebastian Larsson barged Ramires off the ball in front of goal. Upset by the decision, an irate Ramires was lucky to escape punishment moments later when he clearly elbowed Larsson in full view of the referee.

Chelsea started the second half like they did the first, and a brisk counter-attack ended with Eto'o shooting narrowly past the post. With half an hour remaining, José brought on Demba Ba. However, the on-form Senegalese striker could not find his range, slicing horribly wide from Willian's cut-back.

As the half wore on, Chelsea started to run out of ideas. Their play became increasingly desperate and disjointed as a confident Mannone dealt with everything that came his way.

Chelsea's all-out commitment to attack and seek a winner left them exposed on the break, and they paid the ultimate price as César Azpilicueta's slip let in Altidore down the right. The Spanish left-back slid in to try to dispossess the American, and in doing so, was ruled to have brought him down. Former Chelsea and Italian international forward, Borini, keeping his cool, slotted the ball past Schwarzer to send the visiting Sunderland fans into raptures.

Chelsea substitute, André Schurrle, responded with a dipping shot from 30 yards, which again saw Mannone produce heroics to tip over before the Italian confidently gathered a Terry header to snuff out Chelsea's last hope. The 'keeper also saved from a frustrated Demba Ba in the ninety-fifth minute!

Towards the end of the game, with only seconds remaining, shameful and ugly scenes of chaotic violence erupted following referee Mike Dean's decision to award Sunderland their controversial, but ultimately, match-winning penalty. Rui Faria, Chelsea's assistant coach, repeatedly tried to attack the official as José Mourinho clutched, first his arm, and then a handful of his dark hair in his frantic attempts to restrain his fellow Portuguese. In fact, at one stage, it took three Chelsea assistants, as well as José, to hold back the raging Faria. Covering the game for the *Daily Mail,* reporter Patrick Collins wrote,

> Typically, José offered an unrepentant face after the game. He declined questions and opted for sarcasm, one of the few dark arts for which he has no talent. He pretended to congratulate referee Dean, saying "I think his performance was unbelievable, and I think when referees have unbelievable performances, I think it's fair that as managers we give them praise. He came here with one objective, to make a fantastic performance. And he did that."

An angry José also blasted chief referee Mike Riley, saying 'It was turgid stuff, a genuinely stupid performance which fell far below the gravity of the event.'

Let's be truthful ... José has never been a good loser, and in fairness, he has had little practice. But this dramatically expensive defeat by the Premier League's bottom club certainly rattled his cage, and that penalty, converted by Fabio Borini, a Liverpool player on loan to Sunderland, was simply too much for the Portuguese to take.

For his outrageous actions, Faria was handed a six-match stadium ban and a £30,000 fine by the FA. However, after an appeal, the last two matches were suspended, but the fine remained in place. The following is José's home record as Chelsea manager immediately after that defeat:

	P	W	D	L
First spell	60	46	14	0
Second spell	18	15	2	1
Totals	78	61	16	1

LIVERPOOL 0 CHELSEA 2
(Chelsea lost 1-3 on aggregate)
27 April 2014

For a number of reasons, this was a huge game of football. Pundits said that if Liverpool – on an eleven match League winning run at the time – won, they would become Premiership champions. If Chelsea should claim victors, they would be back in the title race, while a draw would suit the Merseysiders and certainly give Manchester City a massive boost.

José Mourinho had seriously considered making wholesale changes in the aftermath of that dramatic home defeat by Sunderland, with a vital Champions League encounter next game at Stamford Bridge.

Goalkeeper Petr Cech was struggling with a dodgy shoulder injury, captain John Terry was nursing an ankle problem, playmaker Eden Hazard had a calf strain, Samuel Eto'o was having treatment on a damaged knee, while midfielder Ramires' season was over after he received a four-match ban for striking Sebastian Larsson in the loss to Sunderland.

José was left with a few problems, but in the end, he chose the right team and got the right result which stunned Liverpool who, if the truth be known, never really recovered and subsequently lost the title to Manchester City. José, in fact, chose to make seven changes to his previous game line-up. With both Terry and Gary Cahill out, he switched Branislav Ivanovic to the centre of the defence, bringing in the Czech Republic centre-back, Tomas Kalas, for his debut. Ashley Cole returned as left-back, Lampard, Oscar and Mikel re-entered the midfield sector, and he started up front with Demba Ba and André Schurrle.

Former Chelsea striker, Daniel Sturridge, was missing from Liverpool's attack, but another ex-Blues star, Glen Johnson, was in.

Liverpool (4-5-1): Mignolet, Johnson, Skrtel, Sakho, Flanagan (Laso Aspas), Lucas (Sturridge), Gerrard, Allen, Sterling, Courtinho, Suarez.
Chelsea (4-4-2): Schwarzer, Azpilicueta, Ivanovic, Kalas, A. Cole, Lampard, Matic, Mikel, Salah (Willian), Demba Ba (Torres), Schurrle (Cahill).
Attendance: 44,726

In their previous five home games, Liverpool had scored their first goal after 1, 3, 39, 2 and 6 minutes ... so it was clear what Chelsea needed to do: keep a clean sheet in the first half and victory could be theirs. And as it transpired, the Chelsea manager got his tactics spot on to keep his side's hopes of an unlikely double alive. With the home side committed to attack, the visitors relied on defending, and it was the latter that succeeded.

By time-wasting and breaking up play, Chelsea denied their opponents any sort of opportunity to get into any sort of rhythm. It was a classic José destruction and frustration ploy. It infuriated Liverpool so much so that, at one point, Steven Gerrard was engaged in a bit of push-and-shove with the Chelsea boss in trying to get the ball back into play, while Luis Suarez stood to applaud goalkeeper Mark Schwarzer for time-wasting. Efficient referee, Martin Atkinson, certainly made it clear by pointing to his watch, intimating he was adding on time, but he did not take decisive action in actually booking anyone until stoppage time.

Ashley Cole had an early shot parried by home 'keeper Mignolet, but Chelsea were happy to concede possession and territory as Liverpool pushed menacingly forward whenever possible. Full-back Glen Johnson's crisp shot was deflected behind. Philippe Courtinho volleyed Suarez's cross into the side-netting. The well-positioned and alert Cole cleared off the line, and when the ball bounced down off John Obi Mikel, the unmarked Sakho blazed his effort over the top. Shouts for handball against Jon Flanagan were waved aside, while at the other end, Suarez failed to capitalise on a rare mistake by Cole by curling his right-footed shot over.

On the stroke of half-time, with Chelsea under pressure, Demba Ba was not as wasteful. A harmless looking ball was collected by the Liverpool skipper, Steven Gerrard, who suddenly slipped when in possession, allowing the Chelsea to run on and score low past Mignolet in fine style.

After the break, Schwarzer produced a terrific diving save to keep out a first-time effort from Joe Allen, which was followed by an even better stop by Mignolet who denied André Schurrle.

Gerrard tried his utmost to make up for his mistake and redress the balance, but twice in quick succession, the England man found Schwarzer with direct and well-struck shots from outside the area, and once with a deliberate header from inside it.

Substitute Daniel Sturridge, returning to action after a hamstring injury, never really looked like breaking through Chelsea's thick blue line, and after Suarez's late volley was punched over by Schwarzer, the game ended with a jubilant José Mourinho charging down the touchline to celebrate substitute Willian's breakaway goal, which gave his side a 2-0 victory.

Liverpool had 73 per cent of the play. The home side had twenty-six attempts at goal to Chelsea's eleven, with eight on target against four by the visitors. The reds also gained fourteen corners to Chelsea's two. But as they say, goals win matches, and this victory was all down to José Mourinho's brilliant tactics.

CHELSEA 1 CLUB ATLÉTICO DE MADRID 3
(Chelsea lost 1-3 on aggregate)
30 April 2014

After battling it out to earn a goalless draw in Spain, Chelsea were quietly confident of winning the second leg of their Champions League semi-final against La Liga leaders, Atlético Madrid. The other semi-final featured Real Madrid against the holders Bayern Munich and therefore, if results should go the right way, there could be an all-Spanish final involving two clubs from the same city, which was a repeat of the 2012 Champions League final when Chelsea beat Bayern on penalties, and a re-run of the 1971 European Cup-winner's final, when Chelsea beat Real Madrid in a replay or a showdown between Bayern and Atlético.

As it was, both Madrid clubs went through, and Chelsea were therefore denied a fourth Champions League final appearance in six years. It was Real who were knocked out, while Atlético went on to clinch their tenth La Liga title. This was sadly José's fourth successive failure at this stage in the competition, and Chelsea's fifth defeat in seven semi-finals since 2004.

Chelsea (4-2-3-1): Schwarzer, Ivanovic, Cahill, Terry, Cole (Eto'o), Azpilicueta, Luiz, Ramires, Willian (Schurrle), Hazard, Torres (Demba Ba).
Atlético Madrid (4-5-1): Courtois, Juanfran, Miranda, Godin, Filipe Luis, Mario, Tiago, Adrian (Raul Garcia), Koke, Turan (Rodriguez), Diego Costa (Sosa).
Attendance: 37,918

Deprived of both Frank Lampard and John Obi Mikel through suspension, José Mourinho selected three full-backs and deployed César Azpilicueta in an unfamiliar midfield role ahead of Branislav Ivanovic down the right. If that encouraged a greater sense of adventure by Atlético, they found almost instant reward for their enterprise when Koke's corner was headed back out to him on the wing. Then, using the outside of his right boot, the Madrid striker cracked the ball onto Mark Schwarzer's crossbar. It came down onto a post, struck Gary Cahill before looping over and out of play. A huge let-off.

Chelsea tried to inject some composure into their play, but were hustled and bustled by their Spanish opponents at every opportunity. They were never allowed time or space on the ball, while the other end of the field, future Blues' star, Diego

Costa, twice muscled through the home defence before being stopped, first by Ashley Cole, and then by Cahill. Chelsea rarely threatened, but surprisingly there wasn't much to choose between the two teams for the first half hour or so. Then, after a couple of attacks directed down the middle, Chelsea took the lead in the thirty-sixth minute with a goal from Madrid's former pin-up boy, Fernando Torres.

Rampaging right-back, Ivanovic, started the move on his flank, but it was the improvisational brilliance of Brazilian midfielder, Willian, who effectively created the chance. His smart turn, 2 yards from the corner flag, took him away from a couple of defenders. A short pass was collected by Azpilicueta, who immediately picked out Torres who drove in a low right-footed shot, which was deflected past Courtois by Mario Suárez. Torres celebrated his goal like a form of apology, with his palms spread as if asking for forgiveness from his former club.

Unfortunately, Chelsea, usually so accomplished at defending, certainly under José, let the lead slip eight minutes later. Ashley Cole winced when he saw the replays of the equaliser because he made a fatal mistake in assuming John Terry was going to clear Juanfran's cutback. Unfortunately, the centre-back could not adjust his feet quick enough, and with Cole slow to react, Adrián Lopez pounced to drive his shot into the ground, the ball gathering enough momentum off the turf to loop into the net. Atlético then took control and looked comfortable as Chelsea back-pedalled, conceding a number of free-kicks, thankfully, quite a distance away from Schwarzer's goal.

José's first response to the equaliser came after fifty-three minutes, when he took Cole off and brought on Samuel Eto'o, hinting that Chelsea would now have to start playing with greater adventure. They did just that, but it meant leaving gaps at the back for their opponents to exploit, while at the same time, certain players continued to contribute to the team's downfall.

Two minutes after Eto'o had stepped onto the pitch, he saw Atlético's 'keeper, Thibaut Courtois, on loan from Stamford Bridge, keep out a thumping header from Terry with a save that José later described as 'impossible'.

On the hour mark, Eto'o, helping out in defence, clattered into Diego Costa following an Atlético corner. The challenge was clumsy in the extreme, giving Italian referee, Nicola Rizzoli, no option but to award a penalty. Costa was shown a yellow card because of the amount of time he took with the spot kick, but he eventually placed the ball high into the net, past Mark Schwarzer, as though immune to nerves.

Shortly after Costa's decisive penalty conversion, a header from David Luiz came back into play off the Courtios's post. But, when Atlético's Koko, by far the game's best player, hit the woodwork in the seventy-second minute, Arda Turan was on the spot to head the rebound past Schwarzer to confirm his team's place in an all-Madrid final. It also took Atlético into their first European Cup/Champions League final for forty years.

Atlético were good value for their victory, and Argentine manager, Diego Simone said afterwards, 'When we went behind, I wasn't worried, because I knew we would score at least once.' Deflated Chelsea boss, José Mourinho, refused to criticise his players for the defeat, saying that his side could not have given much more, but he felt they were the better side up until Atlético went ahead: 'I think until the penalty they were not the best team,' he told Sky Sports. However, ex-Chelsea midfielder, Michael Ballack, believed the team lacked creativity, saying,

> We had more possession, created more chances, scored a great goal but we conceded a poor one. The penalty was a killer and there was only one team in it after that, although in the second half, one minute decided everything. Atlético's goalkeeper made an impossible save from Terry's header and in the same minute came the penalty. Atlético, with a high morale, knew that with half an hour to go they had the game under control. They are a very good side and what they are doing in the Spanish League is fantastic and I congratulate them.

A day after this set-back, José insisted that he was pleased with how Chelsea had performed during the season, and predicted a big improvement next term.

> Next season will be better than this. Hopefully we can bring in a couple of new players to improve the team, but I'm happy with those we have right now and what they've done.

Asked about Courtois, who was on loan from Chelsea and who pulled off that great save from Terry, José simply said 'he is Atlético's goalkeeper right now – not ours.' The attendance for the semi-final was, somewhat surprisingly, 3,880 below the Stamford Bridge capacity.

ENGLAND XI 2 REST OF THE WORLD XI 4
8 June 2014

José Mourinho was asked to manage the Rest of the World XI for this annual challenge match to raise money for UNICEF. And once again, his chosen team delivered the goods. Determined to win, the Chelsea boss had a huge say in team selection and went for experience straight down the middle of the pitch, selecting five ex-internationals in his starting line-up, with another on the bench.

England XI (4-4-2): Seaman (Theakston), Humes, Carragher, Walker, McGuinness, Shephard, Bishop, Murs, Wilkes, Jones, Phillips. Outfield substitutes, all used: Owen, Le Tissier, Whitehall, Moyer, Redknapp, Cooper.
Rest of the World XI (4-4-2): Van der Sar (Kielty), Sheen, Worthington, Stam, Ramsey, Seedorf, Davids, McAvoy, Del Piero, Byrne, Cabrera. Outfield substitutes, all used: Shevchenko, Renner, Smalling, Richman, Bridges, Compston.
Attendance: 65,574

A magnificent, sun-drenched crowd at Old Trafford saw a rather low-key first-half, when very few chances were created. But after the break, everything took off, and the second forty-five minutes produced six goals, plenty of action, some argy-bargy – mainly involving the bespectacled Edgar Davids and the England captain Jonathan Wilkes – and a handful of yellow cards.

It was certainly an early evening of total commitment from all thirty-six players. The professionals who took the field were goalkeepers Edwin Van der Sar and David Seaman, Ukraine's Andrei Shevchenko, ex England stars Matt Le Tissier, Des Walker, Jamie Carragher, Kevin Phillips and Jamie Redknapp, Italian forward Allesandro Del Piero, the Dutch midfield duo of Edgar Davids and Clarence Seedorf and former Manchester United centre-back, Jaap Stam.

Among the 'celebs' who took the field, were Santiago Cabrera (Aramis from the TV series, *The Three Musketeers*), comedians John Bishop, Kevin Bridges, Patrick Kielty, Paddy McGuinness and Jack Whitehall, TV presenters Ben Shephard, Jamie Theakston and Jonathan Wilkes, actors Martin Compston, James McAvoy, Stephen Moyer (*True Blood*), Jeremy Renner, Adam Richman and Sam Worthington, TV chef Gordon Ramsay, and from the world of music, Mark Owen (Take That),

Marvin Humes (JLS), Olly Murs (*The X Factor*), Nicky Byrne (Westlife) and Danny Jones (McFly). A huge amount of money was raised on the day – £4,233,099 – and this was subsequently doubled by the UK government, making it a bumper payout for UNICEF of almost £8.5 million.

As for the match itself, neither goalkeeper was troubled unduly in the first period. Phillips had the best chance for England, heading tamely into the arms of goalkeeper van der Sar from close range. Two minutes after the interval, José's team took the lead. A smart move down the right ended with Seedorf smashing home a right-foot rocket high past goalkeeper Theakston.

The lead was doubled on sixty-nine minutes, when former Leeds United FA Youth Cup winner, Byrne, chipped home from the edge of the penalty-area after 'keeper, Theakston, dithered and dallied and failed to clear his lines following a routine back-pass. But Sam Allardyce, manager of the England team, urged his players forward and, in the seventy-fifth minute, midfield substitute Redknapp, steadied himself, took aim and netted with a superb swerving 25-yarder to cut England's lead by half.

Seven minutes later, it was all-square when full-back Compston conceded a penalty, allowing Phillips to tuck away his twice-taken spot-kick with consummate ease. But José's side had more to give and with time running out, Seedorf set off on a 40-yard run, before exchanging passes and firing low past Theakston to make it 3-2. The same player completed his hat-trick with a well-taken header from Santiago Cabrera's precise, inch-perfect right-wing cross right at the death.

Appropriately, Jaap Stam was voted 'Man of the Match' on his old 'stamping' ground.

José's Managerial Record:

Club	Time in Office	P	W	D	L
Benfica	20 Sept 2000 – 5 Dec 2000	11	6	3	2
Uniao	12 July 2001 – 23 Jan 2002	20	9	7	4
FC Porto	23 Jan 2002 – 26 May 2004	127	91	21	15
Chelsea	2 June 2004 – 17 Sept 2007	185	124	40	21
Inter Milan	2 June 2008 – 28 May 2010	108	67	26	15
Real Madrid	31 May 2010 – 1 June 2013	178	128	28	22
Chelsea	3 June 2013 – to present	57	35	10	12
Rest of World	8 June 2014 (one game)	1	1	0	0
Totals	20 Sept 2000 – mid-June 2014	687	461	135	91

71.3 per cent win rate.

Chelsea's Premiership Record Under José:

Season	P	W	D	L	F	A	Pts
2004–05	38	29	8	1	72	15	95
2005–06	38	29	4	5	72	22	91
2006–07	38	24	11	3	64	24	83
2007–08	6	3	2	1	7	6	11
2013–14	38	25	7	6	71	27	82
Totals	158	110	32	16	286	94	362

Unbeaten Runs

A first unbeaten home League record was set between 23 February 2002 and 2 April 2011, when José Mourinho's teams went 150 home League matches without losing: 38 (won 36, drew 2) with FC Porto, 60 (won 46, drew 14) with Chelsea, 38 (won 29, drew 9) with Internazionale and 14 (all won) with Real Madrid. This superb run was broken by Sporting de Gijón on 2 April 2011, when they defeated Real Madrid 1–0 at the Santiago Bernabéu Stadium in La Liga. After the match, a smiling José entered Gijón's dressing room and congratulated them on '…a splendid and spirited victory.' His only home League defeat prior to that had come when FC Porto lost 3-2 to Beira-Mar on 23 February 2002.

A second unbeaten home League record followed between 2012 and 2014. This one comprised a 45 unbeaten streak: 31 (won 27, drew 4) with Real Madrid and 14 (won 13, drew 1) with Chelsea. This streak was ended on 19 April 2014, when Chelsea lost 2–1 against Sunderland. This defeat also ended José's two-spell, seveny-seven-game unbeaten Premier League sequence at Stamford Bridge.

Some of the Many Players Signed by José for Chelsea

2004–05 – Ricardo Carvalho (signed from FC Porto for £19.85 million), Petr Cech (Rennes, £7.1 million), Hernan Crespo (brought back from AC Milan), Didier Drogba (Olympique Marseilles, £24 million), Paula Ferreira (FC Porto, £13. 2 million), Jiri Jarosik (CSKA Moscow, £3 million), Mateja Kezman (PSV Eindhoven, £5.3 million), Tiago Mendes (Benfica, £10 million), Nuno Morias (Penafiel, undisclosed fee) and Dutch winger Arjen Robben (PSV Eindhoven, £12 million).

2005–06 – Asier Del Horno (Athletic Bilbao, £1 million), Lassana Diarra (Le Havre, £1 million), Michael Essien (Olympic Lyonnais, £24.4 million), Ricardo Gonzalez and Fabio Ferreira (joint signing from Sporting Lisbon for an undisclosed fee), Ben

Sahar (Hapoel Tel Aviv, £320,000 – signed in May 2006), Scott Sinclair (Bristol Rovers, £400,000+) and Shaun Wright-Phillips (Manchester City, £21 million).

2006–07 – German international Michael Ballack (Bayern Munich, free transfer), Khalid Boulahrouz (HSV Hamburg, £8.5 million), England left back Ashley Cole (Arsenal, £5 million plus William Gallas), goalkeepers Magnus Hedman (with 58 Swedish caps to his name, from Celtic, free transfer) and Henrique Hilario (Nacional, free transfer, June 2006), Salomon Kalou (Feyenoord, £9 million), Nuno Ricardo de Oliviera Robeiro/Maniche (Dynamo Moscow, on loan), John Obi Mikel (FC Lyn Oslo, £4 million) and Andriy Shevchenko (AC Milan, £30 million).

2007–08 – Fabio Borini (Bologna, free transfer), Brazilian defender Alex (PSV Eindhoven, return loan), Juliano Belletti (CF Barcelona, £5 million), Branislav Ivanovic (Lokomotiv Moscow, £9.7 million), Claudio Pizarro (Bayern Munich, free transfer), Tal Ben Haim (Bolton Wanderers, free transfer), Florent Malouda (FC Lyon, £13.5 million), Jacob Mellis (Sheffield United, undisclosed fee), Danny Philliskirk (Oldham Athletic, undisclosed fee), Francesco Di Santo (Audax Italiano, undisclosed fee), Steve Sidwell (Reading, free transfer) and striker Claudio Pizarro (Bayern Munich, Bosman free transfer).

2013–14 – Christian Atso (from FC Porto, £3.5 million), Cristian Cuevas (O'Higgins FC, £1.7 million), Samuel Eto'o (Anzhi Makhachkala, £2 million), Nemanja Matic (Benfica, £21 million), Mario Pasalic (Hajduk Split, undisclosed fee), Josimar Quintero (Barcelona, undisclosed fee), Mohamed Salah (FC Basel, £11 million), André Schurrle (Bayer Leverkusen, £18.7 million), goalkeeper Mark Schwarzer (Fulham, free transfer), Bertrand Traore (Jeunes Espoirs, £1 million), Marco Van Ginkel (FC Vitesse, £8 million), Willian (Anzhi Makhachkala, £30 million) and Kurt Zouma (St Etienne, £12.5 million).

2014–15 – Spanish duo of Diego Costa (Atlético Madrid, £32 million) and Cesc Fabregas (Barcelona, £30 million) and Filipe Luis Kasmirski (Atlético Madrid, £15.8 million), Loic Remy (QPR, £10.6 million).

Fact: In all, during his two spells, and not including the odd reserve signing, José Mourinho has so far (up to August 2014) spent around £425 million on bringing in new players to Stamford Bridge.

In contrast, he has sold players for a total value of £244.4 million, who include the versatile Brazilian David Luiz (to PSG for £50 million), Spanish midfielder Juan Mata (to Manchester United, for an Old Trafford record purchase of £37.1 million), Belgian striker Romelu Lukaku (to Everton, also for a record fee, for the Merseyside club of £28 million), Dutch winger Arjen Robben (to Real Madrid for £21 million), Kevin de Bruyne (to Wolfsburg for £18 million), forward Demba-Ba (to Besiktas for £8 million), Icelandic striker Eidur Gudjohnsen (to Barcelona for £8 million), defender Asier Del Horno (to Valencia for £7 million), centre-back Robert Huth (to Stoke City for £6 million), wide man Damien Duff (to Newcastle United for £5 million) and England right-back Glen Johnson (to Portsmouth for £4 million).

Other players sold, transferred and/or released by José when he was manager of Chelsea include: Marco Ambrosio, Yossi Benayoun, Ashley Cole, Carlton Cole, French World Cup winner Marcel Desailly, Michael Essien, Samuel Eto'o, Paulo Ferreira (semi-retired), Mikael Forssell, Geremi, winger Jesper Grønkjaer, champion goalscorer Jimmy Floyd Hasselbaink, USA goalkeeper Tim Howard, the evergreen Frank Lampard, midfielders Florent Malouda, Scott Parker, Emmanuel Petit, the Russian Alexis Smertin, Tiago Mendes and Argentine star Sebastien Veron, plus another Dutch wide man, Bolo Zenden.

José spent £141 million to over £150 million in the summer of 2014, 'to ease the money situation' to a certain degree.

Players Used in a Single Season for Chelsea

The highest number of players used by José Mourinho during the course of a full Premiership season has been 30, in 2004–05. Here are the seasonal lists of the players called up for first team action by José Mourihno during his time as Chelsea manager:

Season	Total	Most Appearances (maximum 38)
2004–05	30	Lampard 38, Gudjohnsen 37, Makelele 36, Terry 36, Cech 35
2005–06	25	Terry 36, Lampard 35, Cech 34, J. Cole 34, Gallas 34, Essien 31
2006–07	26	Lampard 37, Drogba 36, Essien 33, Kalou 33, Carvalho 31
2007–08	21	Cech 6, A. Cole 6, Kalou 6, Malouda 6, Mikel 6, Wright-Phillips 6
2013–14	29	Ivanovic 36, Hazard 35, Cech 34, Terry 34, Oscar 33

The maximum number of Premiership appearances any player could make during José's two spells at Chelsea is 158 - 38 (2004–05 to 2006–07 inclusive, and again in 2013–14) with six in 2007–08. Frank Lampard appeared in 140 of these top-flight matches (2004–07 and 2013–14). Centre-back John Terry has starred in 138 games, and goalkeeper Petr Cech in 129.

Goals Scored for José

Here are the top ten Premiership goalscorers for Chelsea under José Mourihno:

Lampard 49 (11 penalties), Drogba 43, J. Cole 15, Robben 15, Gudjohnsen 14, Hazard 14, Crespo 10, Terry 10, Duff 9 and Eto'o 9.

A Selection of Great, Outrageous and Infamous Quotes from the 'Special One' Himself

(listed in no specific order)
After winning the UEFA Champions League final with FC Porto in 2004

> Please don't call me arrogant, but I'm European champion and I think I'm a special one.

On his unveiling as Chelsea's new manager in the summer of 2004, he reminded everyone of his achievements at Porto with these words,

> If I had wanted to be protected in a quiet job, I could have stayed at Porto. I would have been second, after God, in the eyes of the fans, even if I had never won another thing.

José claimed Frank Rijkaard had met with referee Anders Frisk at half-time of Chelsea's Champions League tie against Barcelona, in 2005. The claim prompted Frisk to retire later that year

> When I saw Rijkaard entering the referee's dressing room, I couldn't believe it. When (Didier) Drogba was sent off I didn't get surprised.

After Internazionale's midfielder Wesley Sneijder had been sent-off in the 2-0 derby win over AC Milan in January 2010, José said,

> It was a strange game. I think we all understand that it was no coincidence that he showed the red card to Sneijder. I have realized that they are not going to allow us to wrap this title up. But we were perfect. We would have won this game even with seven men. Maybe with six we would have struggled, but we would have won with seven.

José went all literary after AS Roma's coach, Claudio Ranieri, accused him of being boring. He replied,

> Boredom by Ranieri? Is it like Sartre's Nausea, which I used to study.

Never in love with Italian soccer during his two years with Internazionale, he said,

> I am very happy at Inter. I am not happy in Italian football, because I don't like it and they don't like me. Simple.

Always one of Barcelona's fiercest critics, after falling out with his former employers during his Chelsea career, José, unhappy with certain refereeing decisions in the 3-1 Champions League semi-final first leg defeat in Italy, he went on a two-day coach trip to Milan due to the Icelandic volcano eruption in April 2010, and with tongue in cheek, said,

> The way they are, tomorrow we will probably read I am to blame for the volcano. Maybe I have a friend in the volcano and I am responsible for that.

José's unveilings can, at times, be pure theatre. There was no mention, however, of his being the 'Special One', when he was presented to the press after being appointed manager of Real Madrid in 2007, but the occasion still produced several stellar quotes, including,

> I am prepared. The more pressure there is, the stronger I am. In Portugal, we say the bigger the ship, the stronger the storm. Fortunately for me, I have always been in big ships. FC Porto was a very big ship in Portugal, Chelsea is also a big ship in England and Inter was a great ship in Italy. Now I'm at Real Madrid, which is considered the biggest ship on the planet.

He quickly left his Real Madrid players in no doubt about who was boss, saying,

> I would rather play with ten men than wait for a player who is late for the bus.

Finding out that the Spanish journalists also take exception to his outspoken views, he responded thus,

> I live and work in a world where you can't say what you think, can never say the truth. Not being a hypocrite, a diplomat and a coward is my biggest defect.

As modest as ever, after winning his second treble, this time with Internazionale,

> You can't win the treble every season. But I've done it twice and I think twice is quite a lot.

Hitting back at Arsenal boss Arsene Wenger, who claimed that other managers were 'afraid to fail' by downplaying their chances in the title race, José said,

> He's a specialist in failure. If I fail to win a trophy in eight years with Chelsea, I leave and don't come back.

José claimed that Sir Alex Ferguson had unduly influenced referee Neale Barry at half-time during Chelsea's Carling Cup semi-final, with Manchester United, in January 2005. He was fined £5,000 by the Football Association for improper conduct.

> In the second half, it was whistle and whistle, fault and fault, cheat and cheat. The referee controlled the game in one way during the first half, but in the second they had dozens of free-kicks. I know the referee did not walk to the dressing rooms alone at half-time.

Defending putting a finger to his lips during the 2005 Carling Cup final against Liverpool, an action which resulted in him being sent to the stands, José commented afterwards,

> I don't regret it. The only thing I have to understand is I'm in England, so maybe even when I think I am not wrong, I have to adapt to your country and I have to respect that. I have a lot of respect for Liverpool fans and what I did, the sign of silence – shut your mouth – was not for them, it was for the English press.

Blaming a first-leg defeat to Barcelona in the Champions League last sixteen in February 2006, on the sending-off of Asier Del Horno following an incident with Lionel Messi, José said,

> It is not a red card, of course not, and for the second time we have to play 55/60 minutes without a man and the game is completely different. I shouldn't speak about the game, because the game is not a game. Barcelona is a cultural city with many great theatres and this boy (Messi) has learned very well. He's learned play-acting.

Accusing Reading midfielder, Stephen Hunt, of deliberately injuring Chelsea's goalkeeper, Petr Cech, after the pair had collided in the first minute of a Premiership match at the Madejski Stadium in October 2006, José stated,

> The goalkeeper has the ball in his hands, slides, and the number ten cannot get the ball. He goes with the knee into his face. Nasty.

Fuming after seeing his side's penalty appeals against Newcastle United turned down, a day after Manchester United were given the benefit of the doubt over a strong injury-time penalty claim by Middlesbrough in their clash at Old Trafford, José said,

> It is not possible for penalties to be awarded against Manchester United, and it is not possible to get penalties in favour of Chelsea. If somebody punishes me because I tell the truth, it is the end of democracy, we go back to the old times.

The circumstances are difficult for us with the new football rules that we have to face. It is not a conspiracy, it's fact. I speak facts. If not, I need big glasses.

José hitting back at Portuguese star Cristiano Ronaldo after the Manchester United winger claimed, in 2007, his penalty rant proved his fellow countryman 'doesn't know how to admit his own failures.'

A player who wants to be the best one of the world, and he already may be, should have the uprightness and the sufficient maturity to verify that against facts, there are not arguments. If he says that it is a lie that Manchester United have conceded some penalties this season, which have not been awarded against them, he is lying. And if he lies, he will never reach the level that he wants to reach.

Shorn of the likes of injury victims Frank Lampard, Michael Ballack, Ricardo Carvalho and Didier Drogba, José cooked up a surreal analogy ahead of Chelsea's fateful Champions League draw with Rosenborg in 2007, saying,

It is omelettes and eggs. No eggs – no omelettes! It depends on the quality of the eggs. In the supermarket you have class one, two or class three eggs, and some are more expensive than others and some give you better omelettes. So when the class one eggs are in Waitrose and you cannot go there, you have a problem.

An early shot at speaking Italian back-fired when, as boss of Inter Milan, he said,

'Zeru tituli' after incorrectly pronouncing *zero titoli'*, which means 'zero titles'.

After Juventus boss criticised his coaching methods in the summer of 2008,

I studied Italian five hours a day for many months to ensure I could communicate with the players, media and fans. Ranieri had been in England for five years and still struggled to say "good morning" and "good afternoon".

Talking to the Italian Press about Didier Drogba after he had left Stamford Bridge in 2007,

I am no longer Chelsea coach and I do not have to defend them anymore, so I think it is correct if I say Drogba is a diver.

Asked about winning trophy, after trophy, after trophy, he said,

We want to follow a dream, yes, it's true, but one thing is to follow the dream, another thing is to follow an obsession … and this is not an obsession, it's just a dream.

Words spoken by José after Calcio Catania president, Pietro Lo Monaco, claimed that he wanted to smack José in the mouth following Inter's Serie A win in 2008,

> As for Lo Monaco, I do not know who he is. With the name Monaco, I have heard of Bayern Monaco (Munich) and the Monaco GP, the Tibetan Monaco (Monk) and the Principality of Monaco. I have never heard of any others.

After Inter Milan had defeated city rivals AC Milan, 2-0, with nine men,

> We would have lost if there were six Inter players left on the pitch.

While speaking at the Doctorate Honoris Causa degree award ceremony,

> It is clear that I will end my career without having coached Barcelona. I confess that it isn't easy to enter on football with the name of someone who is already in football. I feel that with my own son. He already lives under the pressure of being a son of mine. For that, I admire Rui Aguas and Maldini, who managed to live with the weight of that pressure and already did a lot.

When he was unveiled as the new Real Madrid manager in 2010, he said,

> I am José Mourinho and I don't change. I arrive with all my qualities and my defects. I am not anti-Barcelona. I am now coach of Real, but Barça doesn't worry me. My only concern is to grow Real. Barça are great rivals and we respect them. If I am hated at Barcelona, it is their problem, but not mine. Fear is not a word in my football dictionary.

Prior to the second leg of the 2010-11 Champions League semi-final against Barcelona at Camp Nou, he admitted,

> I have to train with ten men. How to play with ten men, because I go there with Chelsea, I finish with ten, I go there with Inter, I finish with ten and I have to train to play with ten men because it can happen again.

After being told he was perhaps the ninth most influential person in the world, he laughed before replying to the interviewer,

> What position is my wife in? Eighth, at least! Look, I'm a coach. I'm not Harry Potter. He is magical, but in reality there is no magic. Magic is fiction and football is real.

In August 2012, José made these two statements in an interview on the Portuguese TV station SIC.

Like me or not, I am the only one who won the world's three most important Leagues. So, maybe instead of the 'Special One', people should start calling me the 'Only One'.

The pressure is not the hardest thing about being a manager, the most difficult is that other people do not have a true image of me. I still hope to continue for many years at the highest level, but I also want to enjoy many things in my life. I am about to turn fifty-years-old, and I feel as if I were beginning my career as a coach.

When a journalist from the Spanish radio network Cope asked him what he believed God thought about him, he replied,

He must really think I'm a great guy. He must think that, because otherwise He would not have given me so much. I have a great family. I work in a place where I've always dreamt of working. He has helped me out so much that He must have a very high opinion of me.

Comments José made about Chelsea's performances at the start of the 2006–07 season, and losing their 100 per cent record against Everton,

Everybody is crying that Chelsea keep winning and winning and winning, so I think to draw at Goodison Park makes everyone more happy. It gives people more hope and brings to the Premiership what everybody was waiting for. Look, we're not entertaining? I don't care – we win. We are on top at the moment, but not because of the club's financial power. We are in contention for a lot of trophies because of my hard work. I am very happy because the club is beating records with the sales of new shirts. I don't sell shirts, but there a relation between shirt sales and the performance of the team. If we perform well, they sell more shirts.

When asked if success in the 2007 Carling Cup final would mean it would be the last trophy he would win for Chelsea before he left, he said,

There are only two ways for me to leave Chelsea. One way is in June 2010, when I finish my contract and if the club doesn't give me a new one. It is the end of my contract and I am out. The second way is for Chelsea to sack me. The way of the manager leaving the club by deciding to walk away, no chance! I will never do this to Chelsea supporters.' (He left Stamford Bridge in September 2007!)

Having been criticised for playing 'boring' football, Chelsea went out and beat European champions Liverpool 4-1 at Anfield, José responded by saying,

> We're not the perfect team, and I'm not saying we are the best team in the world, but I think we deserve a little bit more respect.

Talking about the owner of Chelsea football club,

> If Roman Abramovich helped me out in training, we would be bottom of the League. If I had to work in his world of big business, we would be bankrupt!

When answering questions posed by journalists at a press conference, he admitted,

> I am not concerned about how Chelsea are viewed morally. What does concern me is that we are treated in a different way to other clubs. Some clubs are treated as devils, some are treated as angels. I don't think we are so ugly that we should be seen as the Devil, and I don't think Arsene Wenger and David Dein are so beautiful that they should be viewed as angels.

Talking about Chelsea's young players,

> Young players are a little bit like melons. Only when you open and taste the melon are you 100 per cent sure that the melon is good. Sometimes you have beautiful melons but they don't taste very good, and some other melons are a bit ugly, and when you open them, the taste is fantastic. One thing is youth football, one thing is professional football. The bridge is a difficult one to cross, and they have to play with us and train with us for us to taste the melon. For example, Scott Sinclair, the way he played against Arsenal and Manchester United, we know the melon we have.

Criticising the French Football Federation and coach Raymond Domenech's decision to include Chelsea's Claude Makélélé in a Euro 2008 qualifier, after the midfielder had announced his retirement from international football after the 2006 World Cup,

> Makélélé is not a football player – Makélélé is a slave. He's played the biggest game you can, the World Cup final, and now wants to retire, but the coach told us if he is not playing for France, he is not playing for Chelsea. We know the rules. You are a slave, you have no human rights. Pavel Nedved, Paul Scholes, Luis Figo have all retired from international football. With the Czechs, England and Portugal it is ok, but France? They don't have liberty. It is unbelievable. Makélélé is not a footballer, he is a slave. He has no human rights, no right to choice or liberty, so he is a slave. But the rules are there, so what can we do?

His thoughts on Andriy Shevchenko's goal drought,

> I can tell you now, to stop you (journalists) from asking, that as long as he is not scoring, Shevchenko will play.

In general conversation about his Chelsea squad,

> They have to enjoy playing for me and Chelsea, but they don't have to be in love with me. I don't want special relations with just one of them. I hate to speak about individuals. Players don't win you trophies, teams win trophies, squads win trophies.

Speaking after defender Ricardo Carvalho blasted him for not picking him to play,

> Carvalho seems to have problems understanding things. Maybe he should have an IQ test, or go to a mental hospital or something. There are still other things which concern me, not just concern me, but leave me in a very emotional situation.

When asked about rotating Joe Cole, Arjen Robben and Damien Duff,

> Why drive Aston Martin all the time, when I have Ferrari and Porsche as well? That would just be stupid.

Talking during a quiet time in pre-season training,

> Don't tell me one week later that you don't like Harlington, don't like the weather, or the family is not happy in England. I don't want a player who is not totally committed to my methodology.

Saying what he thought about certain Chelsea players' lack of success,

> When you look now at Chelsea players' CVs, it's similar to Porto's players' before I arrived. Nobody won important things. You have two European champions here, Claude Makélélé and Paulo Ferreira. But nobody won the Premiership. No one has the taste of big victories. I told Mutu, "you are already a rich boy, you won a lot of money, you are still in a big contract. So no problem with your future about money, no problem about prestige in your home country. When you go back to Romania you will be one of the kings. But five years after you leave football nobody remembers you... only if you do big things. This is what makes history."

Words used during an interview prior to the FC Porto v. Chelsea game on 30 November 2004, knowing full well what sort of reception he would get on his return to the Portuguese club,

> I would need bodyguards in Oporto. If you visit Palermo, you probably also need them.

Talking generally about Manchester United,

> I saw their players and manager go for a lap of honour after losing to us in their last home game. In Portugal, if you do this, they throw bottles at you.

Reflecting on Arsenal's penalty mix-up in October 2005,

> You have to wonder why they did that penalty. Because they have so many penalties in the season, that's why. They have to do something special and different.

On the Tottenham Hotspur v. Arsenal Premiership match, which ended 5-4 to the Gunners,

> That was not a football score, it was a hockey score ... in training I often play matches of three against three, and when the score reaches 5-4, I send the players back to the dressing room because they are not defending properly.

Chatting publicly about Barcelona in 2005–06,

> Barcelona are a great club. But in 200 years of history, they have won the European Cup only once. I have been managing for a few years and I've already won the same amount.

What he said before the Blackburn Rovers v. Chelsea Premiership game at Ewood Park in February 2005,

> During the afternoon it rained only in this stadium – only the kit man saw it. There must be a microclimate here. It was like a swimming pool.

Reflecting on Thierry Henry's quick free-kick goal for Arsenal in a 2-2 Premiership draw with Chelsea, in December 2004,

> I am more than unhappy. Unhappy is a nice word.

Annoyed after a 0-0 draw with Tottenham Hotspur, in September 2004,

> As we say in Portugal, they brought the bus and they left the bus in front of the goal. I would have been frustrated if I had been a supporter who paid £50 to watch this game, because Spurs came to defend. There was only one team looking to win, they only came not to concede – it's not fair for the football we played.

What he said about David Beckham, January 2005,

> He is someone I respect as a man and as a player. He is the captain of England and has been a European champion. I have never been critical of him, and reports implying that are incorrect as I've never made comments about him.

Talking generally about the hard-tackling, Welsh international Robbie Savage in 2005,

> Look at the blonde boy in midfield, Robbie Savage, who commits twenty fouls during the game and never gets a booking. We came here to play football and it was not a football game, it was a fight, and we fought, and I think we fought fantastically.

In conversation with the press about Chelsea's London rivals Arsenal, he said,

> Arsenal have won that advantage, nobody gave it to them. By playing fantastic football and by winning matches and by winning trophies, they won that respect that the opponent has for them. Look at the way teams play against Arsenal. They don't believe they can win. They don't believe.

On Chelsea's shock defeat at the hands of Charlton Athletic in the Carling Cup, in October 2005,

> I want to give my congratulations to them because they won. But we were the best team. We didn't lose the game. Ninety minutes was a draw, and it was a draw after two hours. We lost on penalties.

José's thoughts on Arsene Wenger,

> I think he is one of these people who is a voyeur. He likes to watch other people. There are some guys who, when they are at home, have a big telescope to see what happens in other families. He speaks, speaks, speaks about Chelsea.

What of Frank Rijkaard, he was asked?

My history as a manager cannot be compared with Rijkaard's history. He has zero trophies, and I have a lot of them.

Speaking about Sir Alex Ferguson in 2005,

Maybe when I turn sixty, have been managing in the same League for twenty years and have the respect of everybody, I will have the power to speak to people and make them tremble a little bit. People want a storm but there isn't one. I respect Sir Alex a lot because he's a great manager, but he must follow the procedure. I don't speak with referees and I don't want other managers doing it; it's the rule. One thing is to speak, one thing is to shout. This is nothing against Sir Alex whatsoever. After the game on Wednesday, we were together in my office and we spoke and drank wine. Unfortunately, it was a very bad bottle of wine and he was complaining. So when we go to Old Trafford for the second leg, on my birthday, I will take a beautiful bottle of Portuguese wine. But he's a great manager. He is clever and used his power and his prestige. The referee should not allow it. I have a lot of respect for Ferguson. I call him boss because he is the manager's boss. Maybe when I become sixty, the kids will call me the same.

Answering criticism from Johan Cruyff about his style of play,

I don't want him (Cruyff) to teach me how to lose 4-0 in a Champions League final because I don't want to learn that.

On losing 1-0 to Liverpool in the 2005 Champions League semi-final,

The linesman scored the goal. No-one knows if that shot went over the line, and you must be 100 per cent. It was a goal that came from the moon, from the Anfield stands. They (Liverpool) are in the final, and from my heart I hope they win it. The night belongs to them and I don't want to criticise them.

After a goalless draw against West Ham United in January 2014,

The problem with Chelsea is I lack a striker. I have Eto'o, but he is thirty-two years old, maybe thirty-five, who knows? This is not the best league in the world. This is football from the nineteenth century.

After a last-ditch controversial penalty saves Chelsea a point against West Bromwich Albion at Stamford Bridge in November 2013,

The referee made many mistakes during the game, but that was not a mistake. It was clear penalty, even though referee, chief Mike Riley, later apologised to Baggies.

José's comments, thoughts and beliefs concerning pressure

> There is no pressure at the top. The pressure's being second or third.

> If I wanted to have an easy job, I would have stayed at Porto – beautiful blue chair, the UEFA Champions League trophy, God, and after God, me.

> Pressure … what pressure? You cannot put pressure on me. Bird flu is pressure. You can laugh, but I am being serious. I am more worried about the swan than I am about football. Pressure is poor people in the world trying to feed their families. There is no pressure in football … but I'm serious, the bird flu in Scotland is bothering me more.

> I am more scared of bird flu than football. What is football compared with life? I have to buy some masks and stuff – maybe for my team as well.
>   Pressure is millions of parents around the world with no money to feed their children.

José on philosophy and tactics in football

> I always intend to give my best, to improve things and to create the football team in relation to my image and my football philosophy.

Defending his squad rotation policy he said,

> If you have at home one Bentley and one Aston Martin, if you go all day everyday in the Bentley, and leave the Aston Martin in the garage, you are a bit stupid.

> When you just work tactically, in pure football sessions, you can see the way they (the players) can think football.

> When you play another team with the same qualities as you normally, the best one wins.

> You can have the top stars to bring the attention, you can have the best stadium, you can have the best facilities, you can have the most beautiful project in terms of marketing and all this kind of thing. But if you don't win, all the work these people are doing is forgotten.

> You have to win and especially, as I have, you have to win a trophy for the first time.

Spanish, Italians, Portuguese all play football. I don't say they are perfect, I say English football has a few things to learn from them, in the same way they have a lot of things to learn from English football.

I'm not a defender of old or new football managers. I believe in good ones and bad ones, those that achieve success and those that don't.

The negative side of football, the negative side of our society. People sometimes go to football and bring to it the negative aspects of our society.

The only thing I would like is to have more control of the game, in terms of possession.

The Porto players were with me for two-and-a-half years. They believed in me, in my methods, in the way we do it. The next day I go and a manager arrives who works completely differently.

The way I use to develop an aerobic condition is three against three, man to man, in a square, 20 metres by 20.

When you go to the stadiums, the atmosphere is so beautiful that maybe you don't feel so much the importance of the game.

I know all about the ups and downs of football. I know that one day I will be sacked.

If one day the result is 3-3, for me it doesn't change my mind, because it's football – it's normal. What is not normal is that we haven't scored enough goals, despite playing good football.

I think because of the passion of every English player and every English supporter, and every English journalist for the game, most of the game is played with passion, love for football and instinct. But in football, you also have to think.

When you play at home, you need a good atmosphere behind you.

I enjoy the work, I enjoy every minute of my professional life. But I feel I have a lot to learn from English football, and I am completely open to good influences in my way of thinking football. But I also have things to give them.

There's a history made up by each of us that leads us to that final victory. It's that history, in its entirety, that turns teams into champions.

To be the ultimate team, you must use your body and your mind. Draw up on the resources of your teammates. Choose your steps wisely and you will win. Remember only teams succeed.

The moral of the story is not to listen to those who tell you not to play the violin but stick to the tambourine.

General comments made by the 'Special One' himself

Speaking about the Carling League Cup,

It's not the Premiership, it's not the FA Cup, it's not the Champions League, but its still a Cup and we must respect it.

If I made a mistake, then I apologise. I am happy that I'm not going to jail because of that.

I don't have a taste for having ten cars.

I have loved football since I can remember, and I understand the evolution of football and the modern needs of football.

When questioned about his hair style prior to the MLS All-stars-Chelsea game, in August 2006,

It's just a haircut...

I think the best place to work in football is England.

I was nine or ten-years-old when my father was sacked in the middle of the family's Christmas Day lunch.

In my first five years as a manager, I have never had a match where my team had less possession than the opponents.

I won't hold back ... if the competition is absolutely normal without anything strange, I would love to be a good boy and to behave well.

I believe in freedom of speech ... you make a speech and I'll give you your freedom.

Answering a Ghanaian journalist who asked him if has ever phoned Roman Abramovich to see how he was,

Would you phone the President of Ghana?

Each practice, each game, each minute of your social life must centre on the aim of being champions.

Words written in a letter to his players,

First-teamer will not be a correct word. I need all of you. You need each other. We are a TEAM.

At the start of his footballing career, José said,

When you have a father, an ex-top player, and your dream is to be like him, but you feel you couldn't do it, your motivation comes from that point. I wanted to be really big in football. I felt I had some conditions to be a coach and manager. I went to university and studied sports science. This was a real passion and methodology.

The English press, if you understand their philosophy, it was very funny to play their game. Salt and pepper every day.

When I go to the press conference before the game, in my mind, the game has already started.

And when I go to the press conference after the game, the game has not finished yet.

Is José Mourinho the only one who can look at the fixtures and find something very strange?

After the police questioned José over proper health certification for his dog,

The dog is fine in Portugal – that big threat is away – you don't have to worry about crime anymore After the police questioned José over proper health certification for his dog.

If they made a film of my life, I think they should get George Clooney to play me. He's a fantastic actor and my wife thinks he would be ideal.

What others thought, and still think today, about José

Forget the mind games – I like him. I think he sees himself as the young gunslinger who has come into town to challenge the sheriff, who has been around a while. He was certainly full of it, calling me 'boss' and 'big man' when we had our post-match drink (Sir Alex Ferguson in 2004).

José has a very strong personality. He speaks the same language as the players. His success hasn't changed him. He has a few good friends and he's devoted to his family (Portuguese agent Jorge Mendes).

He is a very good communicator and can speak to the players in their own language. He is also very well organized. His team allies structure with individual talent (UEFA Technical Director Andy Roxburgh).

I don't care what he says, I don't listen. I guess when you've invested £500 million, it's a fantastic season to win the League Cup. He's welcome to his opinions, we care about Liverpool (Rick Parry, Liverpool's Chief Executive, talking to BBC Five Live after Liverpool beat Chelsea in the Champions League semi-final, in 2007).

He knows everything about his players – what time they go to bed, what they eat, how long they train. He wants to control every aspect of their lives. I believe that was the most significant day of his life – the day he said to himself "I'm going to prove to my mother that I can make a living from football" – after José quit just one day after he was enrolled in business school by his mother (Neto, Portuguese Journalist)

José prefers to be on the bench so that he can have direct contact with the team. He wants everything – the training sessions, the match reports and the game itself – to be controlled (Andre Villas Boas, assistant to José at FC Porto, 2002–04).

Did You Know?

An interesting insight regarding José's signing of Cesc Fabregas in July 2014: 'It was an easy decision', said the Chelsea boss, adding, 'It took just twenty minutes to convince Fabregas to join me at Stamford Bridge.' The Spanish international replied,

When I knew Chelsea wanted to buy me, I studied the situation well and talked things over with my family.' But then, after speaking to the boss [José] on the telephone on a Sunday afternoon, he flew out to meet me in Spain, missing his son's final game of the season. For him to do that, gave me a real lift. It was a great effort, to come and tell me personally how much he wanted me to sign for Chelsea.

Looking Ahead

Talking to *Daily Mail* journalist, Oliver Todd, three weeks before the start of the 2014–15 Premiership season, José Mourinho said 'If Chelsea kids Lewis Baker (a nineteen-year-old midfielder), Izzy Brown (aged seventeen, who was signed from West Bromwich Albion after becoming the second youngest footballer in Premiership history when he made his debut for the Baggies against Wigan Athletic in May 2013) and Dominic Solanke (sixteen) don't play for England, you can blame me!' The Chelsea manager took these three young English players on his summer tour, and clearly intends to keep all of them training with the first team during the course of the season.

The trio have already played for England, at various youth levels as teenagers, with both Brown and Solanke helping their country win the U17 Euro championship last term. José believes they are, even at this early age, good enough to make the U21 side, and even contest for a place in Roy Hodgson's senior XI.

The Portuguese coach says he will shoulder the blame if these youngsters fail to make the grade. 'My conscience tells me that if, for example, Baker, Brown, and Solanke are not national team players in a few years, I should blame myself,' Mourinho said,

> They are part of a process the club started without me. In this moment, we have players who will be Chelsea players. And when they become Chelsea players, they will become England players, almost for sure. They have to train with us and they have to learn with us. They will learn a lot.

And with José needing to make up his squad with English-born players, Baker, it seems, will be first to break into the senior side, perhaps in the Premiership, while Brown and Solanke are set to appear in the club's Capital One League Cup games.

Another promising youngster at Stamford Bridge (at August 2014) was Frenchman Jeremie Boga. 'He, too, has a bright future' said José. As the 2014–15 season got underway, Chelsea's only regular first teamplayer who was effectively developed in the club's academy, is centre-back John Terry, who has been at Stamford Bridge since 1996.

Moneybags

In June 2014, José Mourinho was named as the second best-paid coach/manager in world football. The annual rich list, which was produced by the French weekly sports publication, *France Football*, clearly shows José sitting in second place behind his coaching nemesis, Bayern Munich's Pep Guardiola. It was stated, at the time, that the Blues' boss was earning a cool £8.37 million a year against the £14.8 million salary paid to Guardiola. Italian Marcelo Lipi (in charge of FC Guangzlou) was said to be earning £8.34 million per year. Dutchman Louis van Gaal (Manchester United) had signed an annual contract worth £7.1 million, while other top-earners included three more Italians, namely Carlo Lancelot, Fabio Capello and Roberto Mancini, French boss Arsene Wenger and England's head coach Roy Hodgson, who was being paid around £6 million.

José Mourinho's senior squad at Stamford Bridge at the start of the 2014–15 season:

Goalkeepers: Jamal Blackman, Petr Cech, Thibaut Courtois, Mark Schwarzer
Defenders: Nathan Aké, César Azpilicueta, Ryan Bertrand, Gary Cahill, Branislav Ivanovic, Filipe Luis, John Terry, Kurt Zouma
Midfielders: Cesc Fabregas, Eden Hazard, Josh McEachran, Marko Marin, Nemanja Matiz, John Obi Mikel, Oscar, Mario Pasalic, Ramires, Oriol Romeu, Mohamed Salah, Marco van Ginkel, Willian
Forwards: Diego Costa, Didier Drogba, Victor Moses, André Schurrle, Fernando Torres
NB: The following players, registered with Chelsea, were officially loaned out at the start of the 2014–15 season: defenders Tomáš Kalas to FC Koln; Kenneth Omeruo to Middlesbrough and Wallace to Vitesse and midfielders Cristian Cuevas to Universidad de Chile; Thorgan Hazard to Borussia Mönchengladbach; Mario Pasalic to Hajduk Split, Lucas Piazon to Eintracht Frankfurt and Bertrand Traoré to Vitesse.

A Bridge Not Too Far

In the summer of 2014, as a handful of star-players left (Frank Lampard, Ashley Cole and Samuel Eto'o among them), manager José Mourinho brought Didier Drogba back to Stamford Bridge – to the delight of thousands of Chelsea supporters!

The thirty-six-year-old striker scored 157 goals in 341 appearances during his first spell in West London, and holds legend status at the club having netted the winning penalty in the 2012 Champions League final. It is common knowledge that the love between José and Drogba runs deep (it always has) and it came as no surprise when the 'Special One' penned these words in a foreword for the striker's imminent autobiography.

> I'm a person who likes to treasure memories, and with them I can tell the world many things. I'm not a writer, even less a poet, but my life has been rich with stories, stories full of extraordinary moments. Looking back at them, I can find only a few special people who I will keep in my soul and in my heart forever. Didier Drogba came into my life in the fifth minute of a Champions League game in Marseille's mythical Velodrome. I'd hardly sat down when that giant with the number eleven on his shirt scored. I remember he celebrated that goal like it was his last and he turned an already hostile atmosphere into a fireball of flares, chants and emotion. The crowd went mad, the noise was deafening. At half-time, I found him in the tunnel and told him: "I don't have the money to buy you, but do you have any cousins that can play like you in the Ivory Coast?" In the middle of this tense qualification game he laughed, hugged me and said: "One day you'll be in a club which can buy me."

Six months later, José signed Drogba for Chelsea for a fee of £24 million. At the time (July 2004) doubts and questions were raised by several people who asked these questions: Why this one? Why not that one? Are you sure he will adapt? Is he really that good? 'Oh, yes, he's something special' said José. 'He's a player I will be able to count on at anytime. He'll score goals, plenty of them, mark my words.' Drogba, of course, became a Chelsea hero and José recalled,

> When the team was under pressure, he would go back and help the defenders; when he felt pain he would stretch himself to the limit and never give up. Then, of course, came what he did best; he scored and scored. Those goals brought him and Chelsea titles and amazing awards.

At the end of the 2007 FA Cup final, following the 1-0 extra time victory over Manchester United, everybody supporting Chelsea went mad except apart two calm individuals – match-winner Didier Drogba and his manager, José Mourinho. After the pomp and circumstance on the pitch, José quickly dashed off towards the dressing room to call his wife – chased by Drogba, who had one thing in mind – to give his manager an enormous hug. They met, they hugged, and they cried. Some scene. José, in so many words, said,

> Didier is a special person and I repeat the word person. I could say player of course – he's an unbelievable one I know – but above all, his impact on Chelsea football club, as an African, as an emperor of the Ivory Coast, as a father, and as a son and as a friend, has been quite brilliant. Didier is a leader, a footballer with immense skill, one of the best players I have managed in my entire career. But much more importantly, he's in my life as one of the best and most unforgettable friends I've ever had. Side by side, fighting for the same cause, that being Chelsea FC, Didier, even when in semi-retirement and with me coaching in a wheelchair, it doesn't matter, he will always be near to my heart.